Not Your Mother's
Fondue

Also by Hallie Harron

Cheese Hors d'Oeuvres

By Hallie Harron and Shelley Sikora

Tomatoes & Mozzarella

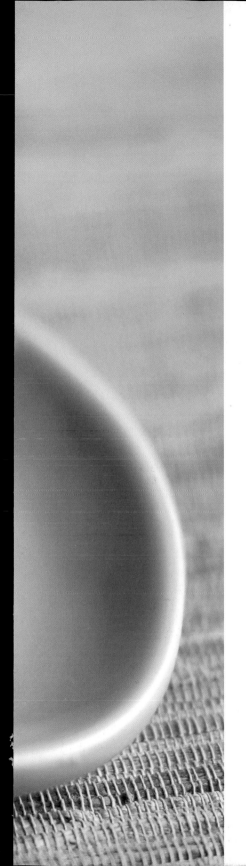

Not Your Mother's®
Fondue

Hallie Harron

The Harvard Common Press
Boston, Massachusetts

THE HARVARD COMMON PRESS
535 Albany Street
Boston, Massachusetts 02118
www.harvardcommonpress.com

Printed in China
Printed on acid-free paper

Library of Congress Cataloging-in-Publication Data

Harron, Hallie.
    Not your mother's fondue / Hallie Harron.
        p.   cm.
    Includes index.
    ISBN 978-1-55832-439-8 (hardcover : alk. paper)—ISBN 978-1-55832-438-1 (pbk. : alk. paper)
    1. Fondue.   I. Title.
    TX825.H57   2010
    641.8'1—dc22   2009050012

Special bulk-order discounts are available on this and other Harvard Common Press books.
Companies and organizations may purchase books for premiums or resale, or may arrange a
custom edition, by contacting the Marketing Director at the address above.

Book design by Ralph Fowler / rlf design
Photographs by Joyce Oudkerk Pool
Food and prop styling by Jen Straus

10 9 8 7 6 5 4 3 2 1

To Serene da Vie,
my California source
of constant inspiration
and guidance

Acknowledgments

Thank you to Gary and Marilyn Litt for your hints and suggestions, and for the music that filled our fondue testing with great ambiance. A huge *merci* to Jay and Fran London for your meticulous testing notes, and, finally, thanks to all the neighbors and friends in Encinitas, California, and Mollans-sur-Ouvèze, France, who managed to help taste and test all of these recipes.

Contents

Fondue Basics

After almost three decades, fondue is back at the top of the list of home-entertainment options, with all kinds of new and exciting themes and variations. Now is the time to dust off those fondue pots, call friends to come over, and prepare some imaginative dippers for the vast variety of fondues you can make at home.

Before jumping into the recipes, here are few historical notes, as well as some tips to make you an instant expert in the field of fondue. Read on for a look at how to select everything you'll need to get started, from pots to dippers, as well as suggestions on how to round out the meal with side dishes and complementary beverages.

Where and When Did the Meltdown Begin?

Historians are in a quandary. Was it the sixteenth-century siege in Zurich, when famine led to fondue out of necessity, or was it the thrifty eighteenth-century Swiss housewives who were looking for a creative way to use stale bread, leftover wine, and cheese scraps? Whenever the actual first melting down of cheese and wine took place, generations later we can all be grateful it happened, because fondue is with us now and is here to stay.

We do know that some of the best early fondues were said to hail from Switzerland's canton, or district, of Neuchâtel, where there was an abundance of Emmenthaler and Gruyère cheeses, lovely Neuchâtel wine, and, of course, bread. The *caquelon*, a heavy pot, was used to melt and whisk everything together. This produced suppers that were filling and delicious and gave the family plenty of time to spend at the table on cold, long, rough winter evenings.

Since there was usually only one pot per household, it went into the center of the table, and bread cubes were speared and dipped communally. The whole process of participation became so popular that it soon spread to other districts. Today each Swiss canton has its own special version of fondue using cheeses and wines unique to the area. For example, the area of Geneva makes fondue using Gruyère and Emmenthaler cheeses and, often, minced wild mushrooms. Eastern Switzerland uses Appenzeller and Vacherin cheeses melted with strong apple cider in its fondue, and yet another canton, the area surrounding Fribourg, serves a fondue that involves diners first dipping their bread cubes in plum schnapps before coating them with the melted cheeses. Kirsch or other fortified brandies and schnapps are a part of the fondue recipe in many areas. The result of these different traditions gives each canton its own special claim to fondue fame.

Prior to the 1970s, fondue was a relatively unknown dish in the United States. But suddenly in the late 1960s and 1970s, fondue sets exploded onto the scene and became a hot item, especially for new brides. (I know I received at least three of them!) During that era, Americans began to experiment with traditional fondue recipes, and eventually dessert fondues surfaced. As the years passed, though, fondue sets were relegated to garage and white-elephant sales. Sadly, fondue lay dormant for a couple of decades and was considered passé. Luckily, in the new millennium we are rediscovering, with the help of the "slow food" movement, the importance of taking time with family and friends at the table. Also, given today's busy lifestyles and people's strong desire for easy meal preparation, fondue feasts are a simple, inexpensive way to feed a crowd of friends, listen to their tales, and enjoy a casual evening together.

So it's now time for your own fondue set to come out of the closet and get dusted off! Or make a modest investment in a sturdy, stylish new set; either way, get ready for lots of creative meals filled with delicious treats and relaxed fun.

Beyond Basic Fromage

There are five basic categories of fondue in this book: cheese, sauce, oil, broth, and dessert.

Of course, I offer several recipes for classic cheese versions. Look for new combos, too, like rich Camembert and Mushroom Fondue (page 28) and a Red Pepper Fonduta (page 22) featuring fontina cheese. Modern melted-cheese concoctions are in keeping with the Swiss tradition and are extremely popular. The good news is that cheeses from around the globe are readily available across the United States in supermarkets and specialty shops and by Internet mail-order. Ditto on the wines to be mixed into the fondue. You can plan a traditional cheesy feast from Switzerland or you can branch out and try melted cheeses heated with wine and spirits from Mexico, South America, Spain, Italy, Greece, France, and beyond.

Keep in mind that there is a whole world of fondue that goes way beyond cheese. I also offer recipes for saucy fondues, in which a traditional sauce typically used for cloaking meats and vegetables is set in the center of the table for diners to dip into to their hearts' content. Try the Creamy Dill Fondue for Salmon (page 63). There's even a deconstructed pizza fondue (page 70), where you dip pizza crust and traditional toppings into the pizza sauce.

Oil fondues both classic and nouveau are also a major part of the book and should be in every fondue master's repertoire. Spearing tender beef cubes and searing them in oil at the table, with scrumptious sauces to dip them into, can be a wonderful way to spend a casual yet elegant evening with friends. These classic oil-based fondues are simple and require only the cutting up of the "dippers," or meats and vegetables, and assembling some sauces or dips for the cooked dippers. Be prepared to love many Mediterranean oil-based fondues, such as Bagna Cauda (page 80), and even a beef bourguignon fondue (page 96) that will make the long-cooked traditional stew easy, accessible, and great fun for a celebration.

Anyone up for skinny-dipping? For those who are health conscious but want a lot of flavor, broth-based fondues, based on the Chinese hot-pot idea, tend to be lower in fat than the richer cheese-based fondues. These are definitely worth checking out if you like to experiment with Asian spices, herbs, and vegetables, as those ingredients are often used in broth-based

fondues, such as Lemongrass Broth for Shrimp and Scallop Fondue (page 115). For some other interesting flavors, try Provençal Fish Fondue with Saffron (page 112), Southern-Style Catfish Fondue (page 116), or Fall Cider Fondue (page 138).

Last but not least, let us remember our collective sweet tooth. Welcome to center stage the dessert fondue, which is best likened to a young Hollywood ingénue—in other words, sweet, easy, and sophisticated all at the same time. I've left these richest and most extravagant fondues for the final chapter, where you'll find not only the Darkest Ever Chocolate Fondue (page 145) but also a very refined Tres Leches Fondue (page 158) based on the famous cake and a fondue version of chocolate hazelnut cheesecake (page 148). Decadence, anyone? Dessert fondue isn't just chocolate; there are also fruity fondues such as Silky Cranberry Fondue with Calvados (page 174) and Melon Medley with Blackberry Cassis Fondue (page 170).

Caquelon Goes Calphalon: What Type of Pot to Buy?

The original fondue pot, or *caquelon*, was a strong and sturdy beast that sat on a wrought-iron stand. It was made of heavy earthenware, which held the heat well. My guess is that these pots were a bear to clean, especially if any cheesy bits clung to the bottom. Today we have heavy, wide, fairly shallow metal or earthenware pots in basically the same shape as the classic pot. Modern technology has made life easier by giving us a nonstick inside surface, which is quick to clean up. For cheese, sauce, and dessert fondues, these heavy pots, whether metal or earthenware, are definitely the best. Metal pots are best for oil- and broth-based fondues, as earthenware tends to crack when heated to the high temperature needed for cooking foods in oil or broth.

Be aware that there are a few fondue pots sold that are acceptable for both low- and high-heat cooking. The heat on these pots can be adjusted to very low temperatures for the creamy, more delicate fondues and raised to high temperatures for the oil- and broth-based fondues. Rather than investing in two different fondue sets, if you're planning to go gung-ho into fondue, it's best to buy the one-size-fits-all-uses pot.

Fondue Pot Options

There are a variety of fondue pots on the market to fit any budget. The most luxurious (and actually the most practical) is the electric metal pot that allows for all types of fondues. The heat can be easily maintained and regulated in this type of pot. It is generally called a 3-in-1 and has a metal pot that can be used as a water bath or filled with oil for meat fondues. This pot also comes with a ceramic bowl for saucy or sweet fondues, making it the most versatile of equipment choices. Some brands also offer a pot that has a gel type

of fuel to heat the fondue, which is ideal for even, clean heat.

For the true classic fondue lover, there are still lots of old-fashioned candle- and Sterno-heated pots that can be used fairly efficiently for dessert fondues. Sterno-fueled pots typically come with a diffuser, which can help regulate the heat. The heat of these pots does not get high enough for many of the fondues in this book, however; the oil-based fondues require very high heat and are best suited to electric fondue pots.

Prices vary based on the quality and size of the pot. Smaller pots will cost in the $20 to $30 range. Generally, the more versatile larger pots, with a capacity of 40 ounces and higher, can be found for under $75. Expect to spend from $30 to about $75 depending on your budget and how many different types of fondue you plan on making. Each recipe in this book lists the size of the pot recommended for that recipe, whether small, medium-size, or large. It's not a hard and fast rule, however, so if you only have a large pot and the recipe calls for a small one, don't worry about it.

All pots come with some accessories. One reason for buying a larger pot is that it can accommodate more skewers or forks at one time, giving you the ability to serve a larger group of diners. Metal forks or skewers are generally part of the package. You may want to supplement your tools with bamboo skewers. A few pots include dipping bowls; however, it is a small concern if they don't, as it can be fun as well as pretty to mix and match your favorite little condiment bowls, cups, and plates. Regular household stores and several online sources make purchasing a whole set, elaborate or modest, an easy task. With a decent pot and the recipes that follow you'll be well equipped to become an expert in the art of fondue.

There are several ways to make do without a fondue pot yet still throw a memorable fondue event. If you have a small (4- to 6-cup) slow cooker, you can use it instead of a fondue pot for cheese, sauce, and dessert fondues. Oil- and broth-based fondues, however, need a higher heat than slow cookers can provide.

Tricks of the Fondue Trade

There are a few simple tips to keep in mind when you serve fondue. They will make life easy and help you avoid any potential problems. Keep them in mind as you get ready to present your fondue to guests.

1. Have dipping sauces and other accompaniments, side dishes, extra silverware, and beverages all ready to go before making the fondue. Once all guests and the hosts are seated around the fondue pot, there will be little need to fuss.

2. Have additional fondue pot liquids ready at the table. This is as simple as a pitcher of additional wine, beer, milk, broth, or water, depending on the liquid that is in the fondue. You will need the additional liquid because the contents of the pot tend to thicken up in some cases or evaporate in others as the fondue party proceeds. Avoid constantly having to get up from the table by setting a full pitcher of liquid within arm's reach.

3. Have plenty of paper towels available for the oil-based fondues, as they tend to drip easily and because some items will need a slight blotting before eating. Fondue can be a little drippy in general, so plenty of napkins are a good idea for any fondue.

4. For a small gathering, position your pot in the center of the table. If a fondue is to be served on a buffet table or sideboard, make sure that it is set on a stable surface like a sturdy cutting board or tray. Guests should be able to reach it easily to avoid dripping on themselves or the floor.

5. Fondue is kept over a flame, so naturally it's very hot. Caution your guests to remember to wait a few seconds before eating a freshly dipped morsel. Especially with the oil- and broth-based fondues, you can burn the inside of your mouth easily.

Fondue Pot Technique

1. Patience is the name of the game with cheese fondues. Some cheeses take a long time to melt. Keep whisk-

ing and be patient, and eventually the mixture will become smooth and creamy. With cheese and sauce-based fondues it is very important to thicken them slightly with flour or cornstarch to avoid separation and a gooey mess. Should the mixture separate after it has become smooth, it will come back together if you just whisk it for a minute or two.

2. Wine makes melting cheese easier due to its acidity, so remember that this is a crucial ingredient in cheese fondues. If you choose a sweeter wine for any of the fondues, add 2 tablespoons lemon juice to ensure you'll have enough acidity.

3. For cheese, sauce, and dessert fondues, always use the lowest heat setting available. This will prevent any scorching or sticking.

Fondue Finesse

If you want to really have some fun, try making a variety of your own skewers. This is as simple as buying wooden or bamboo barbecue skewers, spraying them with a little neutral-tasting oil, and rubbing them with spices such as curry powder, Italian seasoning, ground chile blends, and so forth. When ready to use, soak the skewers in a little water or wine and presto! You've got instant flavoring. You can also buy prepared flavored skewers in specialty stores.

Dippers Galore

I like to call the higher-ticket bites of meat, fish, shellfish, chicken, and cheese used for fondue "big dippers." Everything else that you can dip into fondue I think of as "little dippers." Topping the list of little dippers are little cubes and small chunks of the hundreds of delicious savory and sweet breads to be found in bakeries across the country, as well as scrumptious homemade and prepared crackers and cookies. Little dippers also encompass many seasonal fruits that work well with dessert fondues and some cheese fondues. And, of course, remember the vegetable kingdom. Vegetables from around the world can be dipped into virtually all savory fondues.

How Much Fondue Should You Make?

Depending on the richness of the fondue and the appetites of your guests, you can vary the amount from $\frac{1}{3}$ cup to about $\frac{2}{3}$ cup per person. For example, if the fondue has lots of luscious cream and/or butter, you will probably want to make a smaller quantity or serve more guests with the same amount of fondue. Chocolate fondues are rarely left over no matter how rich or how much you prepare, so plan according to your guests' passions. When a recipe calls for a dipping sauce, a few tablespoons per person is usually plenty.

As far as the dippers go, in general, count on serving 4 to 6 ounces of meat, fish, or poultry per person. This is actually a generous amount when cut into small separate cubes. For sanitary reasons, keep raw meats, poultry, and fish separated from other foods to be dipped. When serving bread cubes, figure about 1 cup of bread cubes per person. Generally, you can plan for about 1 cup of assorted vegetables per person. For dessert fondues, a few sweet biscuits or cookies, several cake cubes, and several berries will satisfy most people's sweet tooth, although extra sweet dippers seldom go uneaten.

Significant Side Dishes

Although the savory fondues can proudly stand alone as a meal, you may also want to serve a simple, crisp salad or other side dishes, either alongside the fondue or after it. Something as simple as a tray of sliced summer tomatoes or a platter of lettuces to accompany a cheese fondue is an easy combination that will help balance the cheese's richness. Or one might choose a starchy accompaniment to the oil-based fondues that involve dipping meat or seafood, like oven fries or potato salad. I sometimes serve rice with the broth-based fondues, so that you can pour some broth over it at the end to make soup.

Sip and Dip

What's best to drink with fondue? That's easy—almost anything liquid that you and your guests like! If you want to go with wine, try serving the wine that is in the fondue or any wines that you would normally serve with the kind of cuisine your fondue fits into. The same principle goes for beer. Punches, sangria, and wine coolers are lovely with fondue as well, as they can be served in casual pitchers and easily refilled. Pitchers of iced tea or herbal tisanes to match the cuisine are also a good idea, as are juices and flavored waters. Whatever you choose, keep it casual, in keeping with the general theme of no-fuss and easy.

To sum up, fondue parties are fun, fast, and frenzy-free. Armed with the above tips and advice, you'll be fully equipped for year-round fondue feasts. *Bon appétit!*

Cheesy Goodness

Cheesy Goodness

Lots of Garlic 'n' Cheese Fondue

ZAKUSKI, THE SMALL APPETIZER PLATE offered before a meal in both Russian and Georgian cuisine, sometimes includes a garlicky cheese that is the inspiration for this hearty fondue. To enhance the Russian theme, serve small glasses of iced vodka along with other beverages and dark brown bread for dipping. ● *Serves 4 (Makes 2½ cups)*

FONDUE POT: Large
DIPPERS: Cubes of dark brown rye or other multigrain bread, steamed potato chunks

5 garlic cloves, finely minced
2 cups milk
8 ounces Havarti cheese, cubed
3 scallions (white and green parts), finely chopped
Sea salt and freshly ground black pepper to taste
2 tablespoons cornstarch
¼ cup heavy cream, plus more as needed

1. Place the garlic, milk, and cheese in a large fondue pot and heat to a simmer. Simmer for 15 minutes on the lowest heat setting. Stir in the scallions and season with salt and pepper.

2. Place the cornstarch and cream in a small bowl and stir to dissolve. Whisk the mixture into the fondue and stir until thickened.

3. Serve on the lowest possible heat setting, thinning as needed with additional cream.

Classic Swiss Cheese Fondue

BACK IN EIGHTEENTH-CENTURY SWITZERLAND, where wine and cheese were household staples, the town of Neuchâtel was immortalized with its *caquelon* or fondue pot. To keep our modern version of this fondue honest and authentic, be sure to use both Gruyère and Emmenthaler, or use French Neufchâtel cheese, to substitute for one or both, if you can find it. (French Neufchâtel is a soft cheese with a rind from Normandy; it is not the same as the cream cheese–like American Neufchâtel.) ● *Serves 6 (Makes 3½ cups)*

FONDUE POT: Large

DIPPERS: French bread cubes, seasonal raw or steamed vegetables such as broccoli florets, carrot sticks, or celery sticks

1 cup dry white wine

⅔ cup heavy cream

2 garlic cloves, minced

1 tablespoon all-purpose flour

2 teaspoons dry mustard

Pinch of nutmeg

8 ounces Gruyère cheese, cubed

8 ounces Emmenthaler cheese, cubed

2 tablespoons cherry liqueur

Freshly ground black pepper to taste

1. Heat the wine, cream, garlic, flour, mustard, and nutmeg in a large fondue pot over low heat. When the mixture begins to boil, simmer for 5 minutes or until very slightly thickened.

2. Stir in the cheeses and the liqueur and season with pepper. Heat, stirring frequently to keep the mixture from sticking to the bottom.

3. When the cheese has melted and the mixture is thick and creamy, serve, being sure to keep the heat setting at the lowest level.

Goat Cheese Fondudo

A BIG THANKS TO JEFF SMEDSTAD, the proprietor of the Elote Café in Sedona, Arizona, who serves a version of this as "fundido." It translates into a gorgeous fondue that will satisfy all fans of goat cheese and Mexican food. ● *Serves 8 (Makes 4 cups)*

FONDUE POT: Large

DIPPERS: Jicama strips, green mango slices, pineapple wedges, papaya chunks, tortilla chips

2 tablespoons canola oil
¼ cup diced yellow onion
2 fresh serrano chiles, seeded and thinly sliced
2 garlic cloves, thinly sliced
Sea salt and freshly ground black pepper to taste
1 medium-size tomato, diced
6 small tomatillos, diced
8 ounces mild goat cheese
One 15-ounce container Mexican crema or sour cream
1 small bunch fresh cilantro, minced

1. Heat the oil in a large fondue pot over medium heat. Add the onion, chiles, and garlic. Season with salt and pepper and sauté for about 5 minutes, or until lightly browned.

2. Reduce the heat to medium-low and stir in the tomato, tomatillos, cheese, and crema. Stir frequently until the cheese is melted and the fondue is smooth and creamy.

3. Stir in the cilantro. Serve the fondue over low heat.

Danish Dilled Havarti Fondue

THIS SEMISOFT CHEESE, developed on an experimental farm in Denmark of the same name, makes a great fondue when spiked with aquavit, also found all over Scandinavia. If you like caraway, then you'll love the subtle flavor of the spice in the liquor. You can intensify this flavor by adding a shake of caraway seeds to the fondue or by using Havarti cheese with caraway.

● Serves 6 (Makes 3 cups)

FONDUE POT: Large
DIPPERS: Crisp-tender steamed green beans, toasted bread,
  Swedish crisp crackers, traditional *flatbrod*

8 ounces dill-flavored Havarti cheese, cubed
One 8-ounce package cream cheese, cubed
3 tablespoons aquavit
2 teaspoons dried dill weed
½ teaspoon freshly ground black pepper
¼ teaspoon cayenne pepper

1. Place the cheeses, aquavit, dill weed, black pepper, and cayenne in a large fondue pot and heat over medium-low heat. Stir frequently until the fondue is smooth.

2. Serve immediately over low heat.

Raclette Fondue

LEGEND HAS IT that in days gone by, when the grape pickers were camping in the vineyards of the French-speaking Swiss Alps, one of them stabbed a large hunk of strong cheese and heated it over the campfire. As it melted, he scraped it off and ate a hearty and delicious meal of cheese, bread, and the local wine from the vineyard. *Voilà*—the discovery of melted raclette! Today the cheese is usually melted on a special raclette grill and then scraped onto potatoes, little cornichon or gherkin pickles, and bread. This version, done in a fondue pot, is easy to prepare for a crowd and uses the same traditional ingredients.

Serves 4 (Makes 2 cups)

FONDUE POT: Large

DIPPERS: Roasted white and red potato cubes or wedges, gherkins, baguette cubes, walnut halves, apple wedges

½ cup milk
½ cup heavy cream
8 ounces raclette cheese, cubed
1 tablespoon cornstarch
2 tablespoons dry white wine
2 tablespoons minced fresh chives

1. Place the milk and cream in a large fondue pot and heat over medium-low heat. When the mixture begins to simmer, stir in the cheese and whisk until the cheese melts. It will become stringy as it melts.

2. In a small bowl, stir together the cornstarch and wine. Whisk the mixture into the fondue and stir until the fondue is smooth and thick.

3. Sprinkle the top of the fondue with the chives and serve over low heat.

Blushin' Bunny Fondue

THIS FIRST COUSIN of Welsh rabbit (also known as Welsh rarebit) shares a little of the name as well as the beer and cheddar cheese. This version, though, is inspired by tomato soup and has a lovely rosy color that is made even more intense by the addition of sun-dried tomatoes.

● *Serves 6 (Makes 4 cups)*

FONDUE POT: Large
DIPPERS: White, whole-wheat, and rye-toast triangles;
   cherry tomatoes; cucumber spears

2 tablespoons unsalted butter
2 tablespoons all-purpose flour
12 ounces dark beer
⅓ cup oil-packed sun-dried tomatoes, cut into julienne strips
1 tablespoon brown mustard
1 teaspoon Worcestershire sauce
¼ teaspoon cayenne pepper
8 ounces sharp cheddar cheese, shredded
3 ounces Muenster cheese, shredded
2 tablespoons cornstarch
⅔ cup heavy cream

1. Melt the butter and flour in a large fondue pot over medium heat, stirring frequently, for 3 minutes.

2. Stir in the beer, sun-dried tomatoes, mustard, Worcestershire sauce, and cayenne and heat to a simmer. Cook for 10 minutes over low heat. Stir in the cheeses and whisk until melted.

3. In a small bowl, dissolve the cornstarch in the cream and whisk the mixture into the fondue until it is smooth, creamy, and thick.

4. Serve on the lowest heat setting.

Fondue Renversée

CHEESE IS THE STAR of this fondue, although it's just a small part of the ingredients in the pot! Instead, cheeses are used as the dippers, with a variety of goat cheeses in various stages of ripeness, along with young and aged Pecorino Romano and various types of mozzarella. The *salsa rosa* in the pot is so versatile that almost any firm cheese you fancy can be used.

● *Serves 6 (Makes 3 cups)*

FONDUE POT: Large

DIPPERS: Cubes of goat cheese (anything firm enough to hold together),
Pecorino Romano cheese, fresh and smoked mozzarella

1½ cups canned crushed tomatoes in puree
½ cup tomato sauce, homemade or store-bought
¼ cup red wine vinegar
3 tablespoons olive oil
2 tablespoons sugar
2 garlic cloves, chopped
5 ounces dry Pecorino Romano or Parmesan cheese, grated

1. Place the tomatoes, tomato sauce, vinegar, olive oil, sugar, and garlic in a blender and puree into a smooth sauce.

2. Place the mixture in a large fondue pot and heat to a simmer slowly, over low heat. Stir in the cheese and heat until it is melted and incorporated.

3. Serve on the lowest heat setting.

Winey Vacherin Fondue

VACHERIN, A SOFT, RICH FRENCH CHEESE, is a common ingredient in some regional fondues. If you can find it in a local store (try Whole Foods Market or a specialty cheese shop) or from an online source, try this variation, which, unlike the classic version, is similar to a thick, winey cheese sauce. A combination of raclette and Comté makes a delicious substitute for the Vacherin. No matter which you cheese you use, try to include the traditional tiny boiled potatoes as dippers. ● *Serves 6 (Makes about 3 cups)*

FONDUE POT: Large
DIPPERS: Tiny boiled white and red potatoes or potato cubes,
small bread triangles, raw or steamed seasonal vegetables

2 tablespoons olive oil
1 small red onion, minced
2 tablespoons balsamic vinegar
1 tablespoon sugar
2 cups dry white wine
1 pound Vacherin cheese, shredded, or a combination of 8 ounces Comté cheese,
shredded, and 8 ounces raclette cheese, shredded
2 tablespoons cornstarch
2 tablespoons dry sherry

1. Heat the olive oil in a large fondue pot over medium heat. Add the onion and sauté for 3 minutes.

2. Stir in the vinegar and sugar, reduce the heat to low, and stir in the white wine. Bring to a simmer and cook until the onion is very soft, 5 to 7 minutes.

3. Stir in the cheese until it has melted into the fondue. The cheese may appear to be "ropey."

4. Stir together the cornstarch and sherry in a small bowl. Whisk the mixture into the fondue and stir until it is smooth and thick.

5. Serve on the lowest heat setting.

Red Pepper Fonduta

BRING OUT THE IMPORTED ITALIAN fontina cheese for this melted meal. Serve with a rich Chianti and a crisp salad of greens seasoned only with your best olive oil, red wine vinegar, and sea salt. The rest of supper is in the pot. ● *Serves 6 (Makes 2¾ cups)*

FONDUE POT: Large

DIPPERS: Ciabatta or focaccia cubes, flatbread crackers, crisp raw seasonal vegetables such as fennel, cherry tomatoes, and zucchini spears

2 roasted red bell peppers

12 ounces fontina cheese

1 cup dry white wine

½ cup half-and-half

2 tablespoons all-purpose flour

2 tablespoons chopped fresh basil leaves

Pinch of red pepper flakes or cayenne pepper

1. Place the bell peppers in a blender or food processor and pulse into a fine puree. You will have about ½ cup.

2. Place the cheese, wine, half-and-half, flour, basil, and red pepper flakes in a large fondue pot and whisk to thoroughly combine.

3. Heat over medium-low heat until the cheese has melted and the fondue has just thickened, about 10 minutes. Whisk the fondue continuously as the cheese melts. The mixture will be stringy and curdled looking at first, and then it will completely melt and become smooth and creamy.

4. Whisk in the red pepper puree and serve on the lowest heat setting.

Classic Rarebit Fondue

THE WELSH CLASSIC known as *cas pali*, or rarebit, actually translates to "rare or lightly cooked" and "small or bit," referring to the dippers. That said, do we dare try a spicy twist on this Sunday supper favorite? Chile pepper–spiked cheddar is a splendid modern touch, and the resulting light orange color is extremely appealing. ● *Serves 4 (Makes 1½ cups)*

FONDUE POT: Large
DIPPERS: Pretzels, toasted English muffin cubes, small toast triangles, cherry tomatoes, quartered hard-boiled eggs

8 ounces cheddar cheese with chiles, cubed
½ cup dark beer
1 teaspoon Dijon mustard
½ teaspoon sea salt
1 tablespoon cornstarch
2 tablespoons milk

1. Place the cheese, beer, mustard, and salt in a large fondue pot and heat over the lowest heat setting until the cheese melts and the mixture is smooth, about 10 minutes.

2. In a small bowl, dissolve the cornstarch in the milk and stir the mixture into the fondue. Whisk until thickened, about 45 seconds.

3. Serve immediately over low heat.

Fondue Normande with Cheddar and Calvados

NORMANDY, FRANCE, is famous for its heady Calvados, a dry apple brandy, and for its tasty apples. This creamy, delicious fondue uses both of these elements, as well as savory cheddar cheese. Use any type of firm, ripe apple in the fondue. ● *Serves 6 to 8 (Makes 4 cups)*

FONDUE POT: Large

DIPPERS: Sweet and/or tart apple wedges or cubes, savory biscuits, baked piecrust sticks

1 small white onion, minced

1 small unpeeled apple, grated

1 tablespoon canola oil

2 tablespoons all-purpose flour

½ teaspoon ground mace

2 cups sparkling apple cider

1 pound white cheddar cheese, cubed

3 tablespoons Calvados or apple liqueur

4½ teaspoons cornstarch dissolved in 3 tablespoons cold water

1. Place the onion, apple, and oil in a large fondue pot and heat over medium heat. Cook for about 5 minutes, or until the onion starts to brown. Stir in the flour and mace.

2. Whisk in the apple cider, and heat to a simmer. Add the cheese and melt over very low heat, stirring, for about 10 minutes.

3. Stir in the Calvados and cornstarch and cook until the fondue is thick and smooth, about 5 minutes. Serve immediately over low heat.

Blue Cheese and Walnut Fondue

A**RE YOU A ROQUEFORT FAN?** Try this rich fondue using cave-aged raw-milk blue cheese. Along with the standard bread and fruit, if you want to go all-out with your dippers, try the ultimate experience of dipping cubes of rare roast beef into the warm fondue. This is the time to savor a special "Saturday night only" red wine. ● *Serves 6 (Makes 2¼ cups)*

FONDUE POT: Medium
DIPPERS: Apple wedges or cubes, toasted walnut halves, grapes, toasted bread rounds, walnut bread, unsalted bread sticks

⅓ **cup walnuts, chopped**
2 **tablespoons all-purpose flour**
8 **ounces Roquefort or other blue cheese, crumbled or cubed**
1¼ **cups heavy cream**

1. Mix together the walnuts and flour in a small bowl. Place the mixture in a medium-size fondue pot and add the cheese and cream.

2. Heat over medium-low until the cheese melts, stirring frequently, 5 to 8 minutes.

3. Serve immediately over low heat.

Goat Cheese and Basil Fondue

THERE IS A YEARLY FESTIVAL in the French Loire Valley village of Sancerre when the chateau's walls are lined with its crisp wines. Huge platters of small fresh goat cheeses are lined up and ready for guests, who sit at wine barrels and eat and drink for hours. What better memory to inspire this fondue? It's a great idea to keep a bottle of the wine at the table for sprinkling into the fondue should it thicken too much as the feasting goes on and on.

● Serves 6 to 8 (Makes 3 cups)

FONDUE POT: Large
DIPPERS: Walnut bread or other nut bread, baguette slices, spears of Belgian endive, small cherry tomatoes

8 ounces garlic-herb Boursin-style cheese, cut into chunks
One 8-ounce package cream cheese, cubed
4 ounces goat cheese with herbs, crumbled or cubed
1 cup crème fraîche or sour cream
1 tablespoon dried basil
½ cup Sauvignon Blanc

1. Place the cheeses, crème fraîche, basil, and wine in a large fondue pot and heat over the lowest heat setting until the cheese melts and the mixture is smooth and creamy, about 10 minutes.

2. Serve immediately over the lowest heat setting.

Camembert and Mushroom Fondue

BRIE, ANOTHER RICH CHEESE, or any triple cream cheese with at least 60 percent butterfat can be substituted for the Camembert, with equally rich and luscious results. A crisp frisée or endive salad with apples and walnuts topped with a lemony vinaigrette will round out the menu, along with glasses of chilled white wine. ● *Serves 4 (Makes 2¼ cups)*

FONDUE POT: Medium
DIPPERS: Baguette slices, small toast points

8 ounces cremini mushrooms
2 garlic cloves, peeled
½ small white onion, quartered
2 tablespoons olive oil
10 ounces Camembert cheese (rind removed), cubed
½ cup dry white wine
½ cup heavy cream
Sea salt and freshly ground black pepper to taste
1 tablespoon cornstarch
2 tablespoons water
2 tablespoons minced fresh flat-leaf parsley or chervil

1. Mince together the mushrooms, garlic, and onion either by hand or in a food processor.

2. Heat the oil in a medium-size fondue pot over medium heat. Stir in the mushroom mixture and cook over low heat for about 15 minutes, or until the mushrooms have released all of their juices and the pan is nearly dry.

3. Stir in the cheese, wine, and cream. Season with salt and pepper and heat over low heat, stirring frequently, until the fondue is smooth and hot.

4. In a small bowl, dissolve the cornstarch in the water and stir the mixture into the fondue, until it thickens slightly.

5. Stir in the parsley and serve over low heat.

White Chile con Queso Fondue

CHORIZO SAUSAGE can vary in flavor depending on the brand, so it's a good idea to keep hot sauce nearby in case you want a more spunky fondue. Have patience with the cheese, as some types of queso fresco take a while to melt. Keep whisking, and if it seems too thick when it has become smooth, add a little more crema or milk. ● *Serves 6 to 8 (Makes 5 cups)*

FONDUE POT: Large
DIPPERS: Tortilla chips, quartered grilled flour tortillas, jicama spears, cherry tomatoes

12 ounces spicy Mexican chorizo sausage, crumbled
12 ounces queso fresco, crumbled
One 8-ounce package cream cheese, cubed
1 cup Mexican crema or sour cream
⅓ cup prepared pico de gallo
3 tablespoons tequila
1 tablespoon cornstarch
2 tablespoons water
Mexican hot sauce to taste (optional)

1. Place the chorizo in a large fondue pot over medium heat. As the sausage begins to cook, stir frequently to keep it from sticking to the bottom of the pot. When the sausage is almost cooked, add the cheeses, crema, pico de gallo, and tequila. Keep whisking as the cheese melts. The mixture should become smooth after about 5 minutes.

2. In a small bowl, dissolve the cornstarch in the water and add the mixture to the fondue. Stir until slightly thickened. Taste and add hot sauce if desired.

3. Serve immediately over low heat.

Sicilian Olivada and Tomato Fondue

A SMALL TRATTORIA featuring Sicilian specialties near San Clemente, California, Gino's serves an exquisite sauce used for dipping chunks of bruschetta. The small mom and pop–run restaurant also features it as a pasta sauce. Thinned with a little extra red wine and enhanced with traditional Italian cheeses, it is delightfully transformed into this Mediterranean fondue.

Serves 6 (Makes 4 cups)

FONDUE POT: Large
DIPPERS: Flatbread crackers, bread sticks, focaccia squares, cooked asparagus tips, fennel spears, cherry tomatoes

One 12-ounce package shredded Italian three-cheese blend (provolone, mozzarella, fontina), or 4 ounces of each, shredded
6 ounces mascarpone cheese
1 cup olivada, homemade (page 32) or store-bought
½ cup red wine
¼ cup toasted pine nuts
2 tablespoons freshly squeezed lemon juice
1 tablespoon cornstarch
2 tablespoons water

1. Place the cheeses, olivada, wine, pine nuts, and lemon juice in a large fondue pot and heat on the lowest heat setting, stirring frequently until the cheeses are melted and the mixture, although still chunky, is relatively smooth, about 10 minutes.

2. In a small bowl, dissolve the cornstarch in the water and stir the mixture into the fondue until thickened, about 30 seconds.

3. Serve over low heat.

Chunky Olivada

Make this tasty olive spread a day or two ahead if you like.

● *Makes about 1¾ cups*

1 cup mixed green and black Mediterranean-style olives, pitted and chopped
½ cup chopped oil-packed sun-dried tomatoes
1 roasted red bell pepper, chopped
2 garlic cloves, minced
2 tablespoons extra-virgin olive oil
Sea salt and freshly ground black pepper to taste

Mix together the olives, sun-dried tomatoes, bell pepper, garlic, and olive oil in a medium-size bowl. Season with salt and pepper. The olivada can be stored in an airtight container in the refrigerator for up to 1 week (any longer and the flavor of the garlic will become unappealing).

Hot Spinach Fondue

FROM AIRPORTS TO STRIP MALLS, most sports bars serve spinach dip, and for good reason! It's a great match for beer or any adult beverage enjoyed during sporting events. For your next keg-and-game night with friends, here's a slightly smoky fondue variation on that theme. A bonus here is that leftovers are scrumptious reheated and mixed with hot pasta.

Serves 8 to 10 (Makes 6 cups)

FONDUE POT: Large
DIPPERS: Small cooked shrimp, bread sticks,
   pretzels, raw vegetables

One 10-ounce package frozen spinach, thawed and squeezed dry
One 8-ounce package cream cheese, cubed
6 ounces smoked Monterey Jack cheese, cubed
2 cups sour cream
1 cup dry white wine
1 large bunch scallions (white and green parts), chopped
Zest of 1 large lemon
2 tablespoons freshly squeezed lemon juice
⅛ teaspoon cayenne pepper
⅛ teaspoon ground nutmeg
Sea salt and freshly ground black pepper to taste

1. Place the spinach, cheeses, sour cream, wine, scallions, lemon zest, and lemon juice in a large fondue pot and heat over low heat for 5 to 8 minutes, until the mixture becomes blended and creamy.

2. Season with the cayenne, nutmeg, salt, and pepper.

3. Serve immediately over low heat.

Parisian Summer Cucumber Fromage Blanc Fondue

ERE'S A FONDUE that is mild and light and, as they might say in Paris, *tra la la élégant.* Serve this with Champagne or other bubbly wine and lots of raw vegetables to keep the svelte guests svelte. Be sure to season and re-season the fondue as necessary with salt and pepper, as this fondue is meant to be low in calories yet high in flavor. ● *Serves 6 (Makes 3 cups)*

FONDUE POT: Large
DIPPERS: Smoked salmon pieces, shrimp chips, cucumber cubes, cherry tomatoes, celery sticks

6 medium-size scallions (white and green parts)
One 16-ounce container cottage cheese
½ cup heavy cream
1 medium-size English cucumber (10 ounces), peeled and coarsely chopped
½ teaspoon sea salt
1 tablespoon dried dill weed
Freshly ground white pepper to taste
2 tablespoons cornstarch
¼ cup water

1. Separate the white parts from the green parts of the scallions and finely mince the white tops. Set aside. Coarsely chop the green parts.

2. Place the green parts of the scallions, the cottage cheese, cream, cucumber, and salt in a blender. Puree until smooth.

3. Place the mixture in a large fondue pot and stir in the dill. Season with white pepper. Heat over medium-low heat, stirring frequently to prevent the cheese from sticking to the bottom of the pot, for 5 to 8 minutes.

4. In a small bowl, dissolve the cornstarch in the water and whisk the mixture into the fondue. Stir until the fondue has thickened.

5. Sprinkle the reserved minced white parts of the scallions on top, and serve over low heat.

Cheesy Lobster Roll Fondue

THE FAMOUS EAST COAST LOBSTER ROLLS hit the fondue circuit here, and you are only five minutes away from experiencing Maine's proud tradition. Serve with a simple platter of shredded lettuce to top the little lobster rolls. ● *Serves 2 to 4 (Makes 2 cups)*

FONDUE POT: Medium
DIPPERS: Toasted cocktail-size hot dog buns or mini rolls; the fondue can also be spooned from the pot onto the rolls

1 tablespoon all-purpose flour
1 tablespoon unsalted butter
1 cup dry white wine
½ teaspoon lemon zest
1 tablespoon freshly squeezed lemon juice
8 ounces sharp cheddar cheese, shredded
6 ounces cooked lobster meat, shredded
Sea salt and freshly ground black pepper to taste
Hot sauce to taste
2 tablespoons minced fresh chives

1. Place the flour and butter in a medium-size fondue pot and heat over medium-low heat for 3 minutes, stirring frequently as the butter melts. Stir in the wine, lemon zest, and lemon juice and heat to a simmer.

2. Stir in the cheese and lobster. Season the fondue with salt, pepper, and hot sauce.

3. When the cheese has melted and the fondue is creamy, sprinkle the chives on top of the fondue and serve on the lowest heat setting.

German Beer Fondue

I F YOU CAN'T MAKE IT TO MUNICH, try this hearty fondue instead. Have an Oktoberfest right at home by melding German beer and cheese in your fondue pot. Along with the dippers, serve a piping hot bowl of tiny whole roasted or boiled potatoes. And, of course, don't forget some Oktoberfest beer.

● *Serves 4 (Makes 3 cups)*

FONDUE POT: Large

DIPPERS: Bavarian rye bread, thick pretzels, smoked
sausage rounds, sturdy raw vegetables

One 12-ounce bottle German lager beer
8 ounces German beer cheese
4 ounces smoked Monterey Jack cheese, cubed
½ cup heavy cream
2 tablespoons all-purpose flour
1 tablespoon Dijon mustard
1 teaspoon Worcestershire sauce
1 teaspoon caraway seeds

1. Place the beer, cheeses, cream, flour, mustard, Worcestershire sauce, and caraway seeds in a large fondue pot over medium-low heat. Whisk frequently until the mixture is warm and creamy, about 10 minutes.

2. Serve immediately over low heat.

Southwest Cheese Fondue

HERE'S AN INSTANT southern California beach meal in a fondue. Side dishes could include guacamole, refried beans, and rice, along with a bowl of lime wedges for squeezing over anything. Bring out the tequila and beer for this fondue party. Canned nopales, or cactus leaves, are readily available in markets with Hispanic sections. ● *Serves 6 (Makes 4 cups)*

FONDUE POT: Large

DIPPERS: A variety of flour and corn tortilla chips, Spanish chorizo rounds, cooked medium-size shrimp

One 12-ounce bottle Mexican beer
¾ cup medium or hot salsa
¾ cup drained canned nopales (3 ounces)
2 tablespoons tequila
1 teaspoon chili powder
1 pound pepper Jack cheese, cubed
2 tablespoons minced fresh cilantro
3 tablespoons unsalted butter
2 tablespoons all-purpose flour

1. Place the beer, salsa, nopales, tequila, and chili powder in a large fondue pot and heat to a simmer over medium heat.

2. Reduce the heat to low, stir in the cheese and cilantro, and heat for 5 to 8 minutes, until the cheese has melted.

3. In a small bowl, combine the butter and flour until it forms a paste. Add the mixture to the fondue, stirring until the fondue has thickened.

4. Serve immediately over low heat.

Blue Cheese Fondue
for a "Chef's Salad"

THIS FONDUE CAN BE SERVED either slightly chunky or smooth, depending on how vigorously you want to whisk the ingredients. Either way, it is a tasty and unique way to serve up a chef's salad. Feel free to add any other of your other favorite ingredients to the "salad" of dippers.

Serves 4 (Makes 2 cups)

FONDUE POT: Medium

DIPPERS: Hearts of romaine lettuce, cubes of cooked turkey and ham, large croutons, cucumber cubes, halved cherry tomatoes

8 ounces blue cheese, crumbled
½ cup plain yogurt
½ cup heavy cream
3 tablespoons minced fresh chives
2 teaspoons dried tarragon
Freshly ground black pepper to taste

1. Place the cheese, yogurt, cream, chives, and tarragon in a medium-size fondue pot and heat over the lowest heat setting, stirring, until the cheese melts, 3 to 5 minutes. Remember that you can serve this fondue either chunky or smooth. Season with pepper.

2. Serve the fondue on the lowest heat setting.

Getting Saucy

Getting Saucy

Alfredo Fondue

ROMANS, A SMALL VILLAGE in the Drôme region of Provence, France, is one of the shoe outlet capitals of France. In the past, posh designers had their warehouses in Romans. Believe it or not, the town is also famous for its mini ravioli. It was in Romans, in between visits to shoe stores, that I tasted this delicious Alfredo sauce that won my heart. How perfect for a Franco-Italiano fondue! ● *Serves 4 (Makes 2¼ cups)*

FONDUE POT: Medium

DIPPERS: Cooked mini ravioli, tortelli, and other small pasta shapes; cubes of Italian bread; crisp vegetables

3 tablespoons unsalted butter
2 tablespoons all-purpose flour
2 cups milk
Pinch of cayenne pepper
4 ounces Parmesan cheese, grated
Sea salt and freshly ground black pepper to taste

1. Place the butter and flour in a medium-size fondue pot and heat over medium heat. Cook, stirring frequently, for 3 minutes.

2. Gradually stir in the milk and season with cayenne. Cook, stirring frequently, for about 10 minutes, or until the fondue has thickened. Stir in the Parmesan and season with salt and pepper.

3. Serve immediately on the lowest heat setting.

Irish Pub Fondue

PATAK'S, the well-known Indian curry spice company, makes a tikka curry paste that is outstanding for this fondue, which is inspired by the curry gravy offered with French fries (or "chips") in Irish pubs. If you need to substitute curry powder, use a masala blend that promises medium heat. Serve with a good quantity of Guinness for the full pub effect.

● *Serves 6 (Makes about 4½ cups)*

FONDUE POT: Large
DIPPERS: Oven-baked potato wedges, onion rings,
all types of vegetables

3 cups half-and-half, plus more as needed
2 cups whole-milk yogurt
1 large bunch scallions (white and green parts), minced (about ¾ cup)
2 tablespoons Patak's tikka curry paste or other Indian curry paste blend
1 tablespoon cornstarch
2 tablespoons water

1. Place the half-and-half, yogurt, scallions, and curry paste in a large fondue pot and heat over the lowest setting until well blended, about 3 minutes.

2. In a small bowl, dissolve the cornstarch in the water and stir the mixture into the fondue. Whisk until smooth and thick. Serve the fondue on the lowest heat setting. Keep a small pitcher of half-and-half alongside the pot to add as needed as the fondue sits.

Creamy All-Season Arugula Fondue

THIS FONDUE MAKES A WONDERFUL centerpiece for a spring brunch, afternoon tea, or after-theater party. Enjoy it anytime, in any season, during any kind of weather. ● *Serves 6 (Makes 3½ cups)*

FONDUE POT: Large
DIPPERS: Seasoned bread sticks, flatbreads, and crackers; celery sticks

2 tablespoons olive oil
4 scallions (white and green parts), chopped
Sea salt and freshly ground black pepper to taste
2 large garlic cloves, peeled
7 ounces arugula leaves
½ cup chicken or vegetable broth
½ cup ground almonds
1½ cups half-and-half, plus more as needed
1 tablespoon cornstarch
3 ounces Parmesan or other aged sheep's milk cheese, grated

1. Heat the olive oil in a medium-size saucepan and add the scallions. Season with salt and pepper and sauté for 3 minutes, or until the scallions have just softened. Stir in the garlic and cook for 1 minute.

2. Stir in the arugula, broth, and almonds. Cover and cook the arugula for 2 minutes, or until it is wilted. Let cool slightly, and then place in a blender with ½ cup of the half-and-half. Puree the mixture until it is smooth and creamy, then place it in a large fondue pot over medium-low heat.

3. In a small bowl, mix the cornstarch with 1 tablespoon of the half-and-half and set aside. Stir the remaining half-and-half and the cheese into the fondue. Heat to a simmer, and then stir in the dissolved cornstarch.

4. Cook, stirring frequently, until the sauce is warm and thick. Serve on the lowest heat setting, thinning with additional half-and-half as needed if the fondue appears too thick.

Bloody Mary Fondue

W ANT A NEW GAME PLAN for Sunday-morning brunches, or an incredibly easy way to feed guests at a fall football party? Here it is. Provision the table with a big bottle of Tabasco sauce and a variety of exotic salt bowls, along with a chilled bottle of vodka. ● *Serves 6 (Makes 4½ cups)*

FONDUE POT: Large

DIPPERS: Celery and carrot sticks, avocado spears or cubes, sourdough bread cubes

2 tablespoons unsalted butter

1 medium-size yellow onion, chopped

1 cup diced celery stalks

One 28-ounce can diced tomatoes with chiles

1 cup chicken or vegetable broth

1 tablespoon Worcestershire sauce

Hot sauce to taste

½ cup ketchup

4½ teaspoons cornstarch

3 tablespoons water

½ cup vodka

1. Place the butter, onion, and celery in a large fondue pot and heat over medium-low heat. Sauté the vegetables for 3 minutes, or until slightly softened.

2. Stir in the tomatoes, broth, Worcestershire sauce, and a few drops of hot sauce. Simmer for 10 minutes. Stir in the ketchup.

3. In a small bowl, dissolve the cornstarch in the water and whisk the mixture into the fondue. When the fondue has thickened slightly, whisk in the vodka.

4. Serve on the lowest heat setting.

Creamy Corn Fondue

THE CREAMIEST OF CORN infuses this sumptuous fondue. It is perfectly fine to serve this on its own or as a buffet accompaniment to barbecue, coleslaw, and ambrosia fruit salad. Any way you serve this fondue, it's a real winner. ● *Serves 6 (Makes 4 cups)*

FONDUE POT: Large

DIPPERS: Mini corn muffins, buttermilk biscuits, grilled scallions, bell pepper strips

2 tablespoons canola oil

3 scallions (white and green parts), chopped

Sea salt and freshly ground black pepper to taste

Two 15.25-ounce cans corn, drained

1 cup heavy cream

1 cup half-and-half

Large pinch of cayenne pepper

2 tablespoons cornstarch

¼ cup water

2 tablespoons chopped fresh flat-leaf parsley

1. Heat the oil in a large fondue pot over medium heat. Add the scallions and sauté for 3 minutes, or until softened and lightly browned. Season with salt and pepper.

2. Stir in the corn, cream, half-and-half, and cayenne. Cook over medium-low heat for 15 minutes.

3. Dissolve the cornstarch in the water and whisk the mixture into the fondue. Stir until the fondue has thickened.

4. Stir in the parsley and serve over low heat.

Puttanesca Fondue

FIRST DISCOVERED PUTTANESCA SAUCE while walking on a side street en route to my hotel in Rome in the early 1970s. I noticed that there were small campfires lit right on the curb and that women in extremely short skirts were gathering, cooking, and eating. The food smelled delicious, and later I learned that puttanesca sauce was actually named in honor of these "working women" who needed a snack in between jobs! ● *Serves 6 (Makes 5 cups)*

FONDUE POT: Large
DIPPERS: Focaccia cubes, baked pizza dough squares, cooked pasta shells

One 12-ounce can whole peeled tomatoes
One 8-ounce can tomato sauce
½ cup extra-virgin olive oil
1 tablespoon Italian seasoning, or 2 teaspoons dried basil plus 1 teaspoon dried oregano
1 teaspoon anchovy paste
2 garlic cloves, minced
¼ to ½ teaspoon red pepper flakes
½ cup dry red wine
¼ cup fresh basil leaves, chopped
1 cup Italian or Greek black olives, pitted and halved
2 tablespoons unsalted butter
1 tablespoon capers

1. Place the tomatoes, tomato sauce, 2 tablespoons of the olive oil, and the Italian seasoning in a blender and puree until smooth.

2. Warm the remaining 6 tablespoons olive oil in a large fondue pot over medium heat and add the anchovy paste, garlic, and red pepper flakes. Sauté the mixture for 30 seconds.

3. Stir in the tomato sauce mixture, wine, and 2 tablespoons of the fresh basil. Simmer for 10 minutes.

4. Add the remaining 2 tablespoons basil, the olives, butter, and capers and stir until the butter melts. Serve over medium-low heat.

Tidy Joe Fondue

THIS CLOSE COUSIN of the Sloppy Joe is great to serve at kids' birthday celebrations as well as to an older crowd that appreciates retro fun. Keep a small supply of ketchup nearby to thin out the fondue as it sits. And if you have two fondue pots, serve S'mores Fondue (page 147) for dessert for a real walk down memory lane. ● *Serves 6 (Makes 5 cups)*

FONDUE POT: Large

DIPPERS: Baked potato skins cut into small pieces, wedges of toasted garlic bread, baguette slices

2 tablespoons canola oil

½ cup minced yellow onion

1 garlic clove, minced

1 teaspoon paprika

1¼ pounds ground turkey

One 28-ounce can diced tomatoes with chiles

¾ cup red wine

⅔ cup ketchup

1 tablespoon Worcestershire sauce

1 tablespoon Dijon mustard

1. Heat the oil in a large fondue pot over medium heat. Add the onion, garlic, and paprika and cook for 1 minute.

2. Add the turkey and cook until browned, 10 to 12 minutes, stirring frequently.

3. Stir in the tomatoes and wine and simmer for 20 minutes over medium-low heat.

4. Stir in the ketchup, Worcestershire sauce, and mustard and whisk until the fondue is smooth. Serve over medium-low heat.

Black Bean Fondue

TRY THIS FONDUE when the urge for earthy and spicy strikes. Mexican *sopes* or other fresh baked goods made from masa are a natural accompaniment. Meat lovers might want to try this with dippers of grilled chicken or pork skewers. This easy-on-the-wallet fondue can be doubled for a large crowd.

● *Serves 4 (Makes 2 cups)*

FONDUE POT: Medium

DIPPERS: White, yellow, and blue corn chips; prepared baked masa
rounds; vegetable spears; grilled chicken or pork skewers

One 15-ounce can black beans, rinsed and drained
¾ cup lager-style beer
½ cup oil-packed sun-dried tomatoes, cut into strips
1 teaspoon dried chipotle powder or ½ canned chipotle chile, minced
2 garlic cloves, minced
4 scallions (white and green parts), chopped
2½ ounces Mexican white cotijo cheese, grated
Hot sauce to taste
3 tablespoons minced fresh cilantro

1. Place the beans in a food processor or blender and puree to a chunky consistency. Place in a medium-size fondue pot and add the beer, sun-dried tomatoes, chipotle, garlic, scallions, and cheese.

2. Heat over the lowest setting, stirring frequently, until the mixture is creamy, about 10 minutes.

3. Season with hot sauce, sprinkle the cilantro over the top, and serve over low heat.

Brazilian Bean Fondue

THIS IS A GREAT MAIN EVENT for a South American feast. You can also use this fondue as a separate sauce for beef cooked in an oil-based fondue. Serve with a pitcher of orange juice to both freshen up your beverage lineup and to thin out the fondue as it gradually thickens. The recipe also can be doubled for a larger crowd. ● *Serves 2 to 3 (Makes 1¾ cups)*

FONDUE POT: Small
DIPPERS: Cheese-flavored or other bread cubes, seasonal vegetables such as
    raw carrots, celery, and jicama and cooked broccoli and cauliflower

½ cup diced white onion
2 tablespoons canola oil
2 garlic cloves, minced
One 15-ounce can black beans, drained
1 fresh mild Anaheim chile, seeded and minced
1½ teaspoons ground cumin
¼ teaspoon ground cardamom
Pinch of ground cloves
⅓ cup freshly squeezed orange juice
2 tablespoons dry sherry
1 tablespoon apple cider vinegar or other mild-flavored vinegar

1. Place the onion, oil, and garlic in a small fondue pot over medium heat. Cook for 3 to 5 minutes, until the onion has softened.

2. Stir in the beans, chile, cumin, cardamom, and cloves and cook for 5 minutes.

3. Stir in the orange juice, sherry, and vinegar and heat to a simmer. Cook for 2 minutes, or until the beans are bubbly. They will retain their shape in the chunky sauce.

4. Serve over medium-low heat.

Warm Hummus Fondue

HUMMUS, a common Middle Eastern dish, is transformed into a heavenly taste treat when served warm as a fondue. Any of your favorite additions, such as sun-dried tomatoes, roasted garlic, and herbs of your choice, will give the hummus your personal signature. ● *Serves 4 (Makes 2 cups)*

FONDUE POT: Medium

DIPPERS: Small pita bread squares; all types of seasonal vegetables, including cucumber spears, celery sticks, fennel slices, cherry tomatoes, green beans, cauliflower and broccoli florets

One 15-ounce can chickpeas, rinsed and drained
½ cup milk or soy milk
¼ cup vegetable broth
2 tablespoons canola oil
1 tablespoon hot chili sesame oil
1 tablespoon freshly squeezed lemon juice
2 garlic cloves, minced
2 tablespoons minced fresh flat-leaf parsley
1 teaspoon ground cumin
Sea salt and freshly ground black pepper to taste

1. Place the chickpeas, milk, broth, canola oil, sesame oil, lemon juice, garlic, parsley, and cumin in a blender and puree until smooth.

2. Heat the puree in a medium-size fondue pot over medium heat. Season with salt and pepper and serve over low heat.

Red Lentil Fondue

TO ADD AN AUTHENTIC TOUCH to this silky East Indian fondue, use homemade or purchased cooked clarified butter, known as ghee. A pitcher of fruity mango lassi, the traditional refreshing yogurt beverage found all over India, and some beer will round out the menu. ● *Serves 6 (Makes 3½ cups)*

FONDUE POT: Large

DIPPERS: Small Indian poppadums, tandoori breads, poori, cooked seasonal vegetables

2 teaspoons black mustard seeds
2 tablespoons unsalted butter
½ cup chopped yellow onion
1 tablespoon minced fresh ginger
1 garlic clove, minced
1 cup red lentils
½ teaspoon ground cumin
½ teaspoon ground turmeric
½ teaspoon ground cinnamon
Large pinch of cayenne pepper
1½ cups chicken or vegetable broth
1 cup coconut milk
Sea salt and freshly ground black pepper to taste

1. Place the mustard seeds in a large fondue pot and heat over medium heat until the seeds begin to pop. Add the butter and reduce the heat to medium-low.

2. Stir in the onion, ginger, and garlic and sauté for 1 minute. Stir in the lentils, cumin, turmeric, cinnamon, and cayenne and sauté for 1 minute. Add the broth and simmer for 30 minutes, or until the lentils are fully cooked and have an almost pureed appearance.

3. Stir in the coconut milk, season with salt and pepper, and serve over low heat.

Tuscan Fagioli Fondue

BASED ON THE CLASSIC central Italian preparation of beans in a flask or bottle, this fondue is a taste of Tuscany in a fondue pot. Add more cheese and broth as the fondue thickens so that it will stay thin enough for dipping. ● *Serves 4 (Makes 2½ cups)*

FONDUE POT: Medium

DIPPERS: Ciabatta cubes, unsalted Italian bread wedges, small chunks of Parmesan cheese, cherry tomato halves, celery sticks

½ cup chopped pancetta
1 tablespoon olive oil
2 large garlic cloves, minced
One 15-ounce can cannellini beans, rinsed and drained
½ cup tomato sauce, homemade or store-bought
½ cup chicken broth, plus more as needed
1 tablespoon minced fresh rosemary leaves
1 teaspoon ground sage
Sea salt and freshly ground black pepper to taste
2 ounces mozzarella, shredded

1. Place the pancetta in a medium-size fondue pot and heat over medium heat. When the pancetta has begun to render a little fat, add the oil and garlic and cook for another 2 minutes.

2. Place the beans and tomato sauce in a blender and pulse into a smooth puree. Stir the bean mixture into the pot, add the broth, rosemary, and sage, and season with salt and pepper. Cook for about 5 minutes, stirring frequently and adding more broth if the mixture appears too thick.

3. Sprinkle the shredded mozzarella on top of the fondue and serve on the lowest heat setting.

Sunday Supper Lentil Fondue

SO THICK YOU COULD STAND A SPOON IN IT" is a common compliment for my longtime friend Ida Lipwich's famous lentil soup. Transferred to the fondue pot, it is a perfect saucy fondue and an ideal meal for an early Sunday evening at the table with friends. Freezing the bacon for 30 minutes before chopping it will make the task much easier. ● *Serves 6 (Makes 4 cups)*

FONDUE POT: Large
DIPPERS: All types of flatbread, pita squares, seasonal vegetables,
   steamed medium-size shrimp, cubes of roasted chicken

6 strips bacon, finely chopped
½ cup chopped yellow onion
2 garlic cloves, chopped
Sea salt and freshly ground black pepper to taste
2 cups cooked lentils (any variety)
1½ cups milk
One 8-ounce package cream cheese, cubed
½ cup chunky tomato sauce, homemade or store-bought
2 teaspoons paprika
3 tablespoons minced fresh flat-leaf parsley

1. Place the bacon in a large fondue pot and cook over medium heat until crisp. Stir in the onion and garlic and season with salt and pepper. Cook for 3 minutes.

2. Stir in the lentils, milk, cream cheese, tomato sauce, and paprika and heat over low heat until the cheese has melted and the lentils appear smooth and creamy, about 10 minutes.

3. Stir in the parsley and serve over low heat.

Creamy Crab Fondue

T HIS FONDUE CALLS TO MIND a rich, special-occasion meal, such as lobster Thermidor, so indulge in as much extravagance as your budget will allow. When you're planning a really special evening, try this with chunks of king crab or morsels of lobster. It's luxury on a fondue fork!

● *Serves 4 (Makes 2½ cups)*

FONDUE POT: Medium

DIPPERS: French bread cubes, celery sticks, cooked fresh
  artichoke hearts, Belgian endive leaves

One 8-ounce package cream cheese, cubed
½ cup heavy cream
½ cup fresh crabmeat, picked over, or one 6-ounce can crabmeat, drained
2 tablespoons freshly squeezed lemon juice
1½ teaspoons lemon zest
6 strips bacon, cooked and crumbled
½ cup chopped tomatoes
1 teaspoon dried tarragon
¼ cup chopped scallions (white and green parts)
Hot sauce to taste
Sea salt to taste

1. Place the cream cheese, cream, crab, lemon juice, and lemon zest in a medium-size fondue pot and heat over medium-low heat until the cheese melts.

2. Stir in the bacon, tomatoes, tarragon, and scallions. Season with hot sauce and salt. Serve over low heat.

Greek Feta and Shrimp Fondue
in Mediterranean Tomato Broth

HERE'S A GREEK-THEMED PARTY FONDUE tailor-made for shrimp lovers. Remember that one man's jumbo size is another's medium, so plan for at least 4 to 8 shrimp per person, depending on what size you buy.

● *Serves 6 (Makes 7 cups chunky sauce)*

FONDUE POT: Large

DIPPERS: Shrimp (see below), pita bread wedges, skewered Greek olives, cubes of feta cheese

2 tablespoons olive oil
1 medium-size yellow onion, minced
2 large garlic cloves, minced
One 28-ounce can diced tomatoes
½ cup red wine
1 tablespoon fresh oregano, minced
Sea salt and freshly ground black pepper to taste
2 cups chicken or vegetable broth
1½ pounds raw jumbo shrimp, shelled and deveined
Yogurt Dill Sauce (recipe follows)

1. Heat the olive oil in a large fondue pot over medium heat. Add the onion and sauté for 5 minutes, or until lightly brown. Add the garlic and sauté for 30 seconds.

2. Stir in the tomatoes, wine, and oregano. Season with salt and pepper and cook for 10 minutes.

3. Stir in the broth and heat to a simmer, about 3 minutes.

4. Serve the fondue over medium heat. Spear and cook the shrimp in the broth for about 2 minutes, or until pink and firm. Dip the cooked shrimp into the yogurt sauce.

Yogurt Dill Sauce

● *Makes 2 cups*

One 15-ounce container thick Greek-style yogurt
One 6-ounce container feta cheese, crumbled
Zest of 1 lemon
2 tablespoons freshly squeezed lemon juice
1 tablespoon chopped fresh dill
Freshly ground black pepper to taste

1. Stir together the yogurt, feta, lemon zest, lemon juice, and dill in a medium-size bowl.

2. Season with pepper and transfer to a serving bowl.

Callaloo Fondue

CALLALOO IS A SLIGHTLY SOUR leafy green vegetable most associated with the Caribbean. Spinach is an excellent substitute for callaloo, which can be hard to find in the United States. When mixed with salt pork and coconut milk, it melts into a heavenly fondue. Add crab and you've got a feast fit for a fete. ● *Serves 6 (Makes 5 cups)*

FONDUE POT: Large
DIPPERS: Cornbread or mini corn muffins, small cubes of potato rolls,
   cooked sweet potato cubes

3 ounces salt pork, cut into ¼-inch cubes
1 large white onion, chopped
3 garlic cloves, chopped
2½ cups chicken broth
One 13.5-ounce can coconut milk
One 16-ounce bag frozen chopped spinach, thawed and squeezed dry
½ cup fresh crabmeat, picked over, or one 6-ounce can crabmeat, drained
Hot sauce to taste

1. Place the salt pork in a large fondue pot over medium-low heat. Cook for 10 minutes, or until the salt pork is crisp and the fat has rendered.

2. Stir in the onion and garlic and cook for 3 minutes, or until the onion has softened and the garlic is very lightly browned.

3. Stir in the broth and coconut milk and simmer for 10 minutes. Stir in the spinach and crab and heat until the spinach is just warm.

4. Season with hot sauce and serve on the lowest heat setting.

Creamy Dill Fondue for Salmon

T HIS IS EXCELLENT served with both raw wild-caught salmon, which you poach in the creamy sauce, and mild cold-smoked salmon, which you just dip into the sauce. Since the sauce takes a little time to thicken, it can be made on the stovetop and simply transferred to the fondue pot when it's ready to serve. ● *Serves 6 (Makes about 4 ½ cups)*

FONDUE POT: Large

DIPPERS: Raw salmon cubes (see below), smoked salmon cubes, cucumber cubes

3 tablespoons unsalted butter

2 tablespoons all-purpose flour

4 cups milk

1 tablespoon lemon zest

½ cup dry sherry

½ cup heavy cream

2 tablespoons minced fresh dill

2 tablespoons capers

1 tablespoon cornstarch

2 tablespoons water

1½ pounds salmon fillets, skinned and cut into ¾-inch cubes

12 ounces smoked salmon, skinned and cut into ½-inch cubes

2 English cucumbers, cut into ¾-inch cubes

1. Melt the butter in a large fondue pot. Whisk in the flour and cook for 2 minutes over medium-low heat. Whisk in the milk and lemon zest and cook, stirring frequently, over medium-low heat for 20 minutes, or until the milk thickens slightly.

2. Stir in the sherry, cream, dill, and capers and cook for an additional 10 minutes.

3. In a small bowl, dissolve the cornstarch in the water and stir the mixture into the fondue. Whisk until the fondue is smooth and creamy.

4. Serve the fondue over low-medium heat. Cook the raw salmon pieces in the sauce for 30 seconds, or until lightly cooked. Dip the smoked salmon and the cucumbers into the warm sauce.

Kathmandu Street Fondue

FIRST TASTED THIS EXOTIC FONDUE as an add-on sauce while eating street food in Kathmandu, Nepal. Now with a little imagination and a light thinning, it has become one of my favorite fondues and always evokes memories of that incredible time of trekking and feasting. ● *Serves 6 (Makes 5 cups)*

FONDUE POT: Large

DIPPERS: Indian breads, poppadums, quartered hard-boiled eggs, cauliflower florets, skewers of cooked fish or chicken

2 cups plain yogurt
3 tablespoons chickpea flour
1 tablespoon curry powder
4 cups water
1 tablespoon sugar
1 tablespoon chopped fresh ginger
1 teaspoon hot chili sauce or 2 small fresh green chiles, minced, or to taste

1. Place the yogurt, chickpea flour, and curry powder in a large fondue pot and whisk to combine thoroughly.

2. Add the water, sugar, ginger, and chili sauce, stirring frequently and cooking until the mixture is smooth and hot. Adjust the taste with additional chili sauce if desired.

3. Serve over low heat.

Parmesan Party Fondue

THIS FONDUE IS REMINISCENT of a thinned-out old-school Mornay sauce. Dressed up with nutty Parmesan, a hint of spirits, and just a touch of red pepper, it is definitely up-to-date and an elegant winner.

● *Serves 6 (Makes 4 cups)*

FONDUE POT: Large

DIPPERS: Cubes of roasted chicken, grilled or boiled shrimp, cooked lobster chunks

One 8-ounce package cream cheese, cubed

4 ounces Parmesan cheese, shredded

1 cup sour cream

2 tablespoons olive oil

2 tablespoons Italian grappa or vodka

1 teaspoon red pepper flakes

1 cup prepared marinara sauce

½ cup half-and-half, plus more as needed

1. Place the cream cheese, Parmesan, sour cream, olive oil, grappa, and red pepper flakes in a large fondue pot and heat over medium-low heat for 10 minutes, stirring, until the cheeses and sour cream have melted and the mixture becomes smooth and creamy.

2. Add the marinara sauce and the half-and-half and stir until the mixture is blended and thin enough to dip into.

3. Serve over low heat.

Avgolemono Fondue

A LIGHT, LEMONY, REFRESHING GRECIAN treat awaits you here. In Greece, avgolemono sauce is used in many recipes and is also made into a soup. When serving this fondue, be very sure to keep it on the lowest setting or just barely warm. ● *Serves 6 (Makes 4½ cups)*

FONDUE POT: Large
DIPPERS: Pita bread squares, cooked artichoke hearts or leaves, roasted chicken pieces, cooked small shrimp

6 cups chicken broth
1 medium-size white onion, minced
⅓ cup white rice
2 large garlic cloves, minced
⅓ cup freshly squeezed lemon juice
3 large eggs, beaten
Sea salt and freshly ground black pepper to taste

1. Place the broth, onion, rice, and garlic in a large fondue pot and heat over medium heat. Bring to a simmer and cook for 15 minutes, or until the rice is just tender.

2. Stir in the lemon juice and eggs and reduce the heat to the lowest possible setting. Cook for 3 minutes, or until the fondue begins to thicken.

3. Season with salt and pepper and serve on the lowest heat setting.

Provençal Roasted Tomato and Olive Fondue

LUCKILY, THERE ARE MANY TYPES of prepared tapenades or olive pastes readily available today, so making this fondue is a snap. Try it with your favorite type of tapenade, or play around with a mixture. I find the ideal combination to be a chunky olive spread with mixed green and black olives. *Très bon!* ● *Serves 6 (Makes 5 cups)*

FONDUE POT: Large

DIPPERS: Small cooked beef or pork meatballs, baguette slices, cubes of provolone or young Pecorino Romano cheese

1½ pounds Roma tomatoes, cored and quartered

1 cup red wine, plus more as needed

1 red bell pepper, seeded and quartered

2 shallots, minced

3 garlic cloves

2 large sprigs fresh oregano or 2 teaspoons dried oregano

2 tablespoons olive oil

One 6-ounce jar olive tapenade

2 tablespoons chopped fresh basil

1. Preheat the oven to 375°F. Oil an 11 x 13-inch baking dish.

2. Place the tomatoes, wine, bell pepper, shallots, garlic, and oregano in the dish and sprinkle the vegetables with the olive oil. Roast for 1 hour, or until the vegetables are very soft.

3. Let cool slightly, then transfer the contents of the baking dish to a blender and puree, in batches if necessary, until smooth. Place the puree in a large fondue pot and stir in the tapenade and basil.

4. Heat the fondue over low heat until just warm, thinning with additional wine if the mixture appears too thick. Serve over medium heat.

Sweet and Sour
Asian Fondue

IN LIEU OF ORDERING TAKE-OUT SOMETIME, try a mostly Chinese-style fondue. Prepare a big pot of rice and platters of snow peas, crispy noodles, bean sprouts, and fresh cilantro to serve alongside in small bowls. Asian soup spoons are handy here for dipping into the sauce. ● *Serves 6 (Makes 6 cups sauce)*

FONDUE POT: Large
DIPPERS: Chicken and pork cubes (see below),
    steamed bok choy spears

1 pound bok choy, cut into spears

2 tablespoons canola oil

½ cup chopped scallions (white and green parts)

1 tablespoon minced fresh ginger

1 teaspoon hot chili sauce

2 garlic cloves, chopped

One 28-ounce can ground peeled tomatoes

2 cups vegetable or chicken broth

½ cup Chinese rice wine

1 tablespoon dark brown sugar

1 tablespoon soy sauce

1 tablespoon cornstarch

2 tablespoons water

1 to 2 tablespoons rice vinegar

½ teaspoon sesame oil

8 ounces boneless, skinless chicken breast, cut into ½-inch cubes

8 ounces pork tenderloin, cut into ½-inch cubes

1. Place the bok choy spears in a steaming basket and steam over simmering water until just tender, about 3 minutes.

2. Heat the oil in a large fondue pot over medium heat. Add the scallions, ginger, chili sauce, and garlic and sauté for 1 minute.

3. Stir in the tomatoes, broth, rice wine, brown sugar, and soy sauce. Heat, stirring occasionally, until the fondue begins to simmer, 5 to 8 minutes.

4. In a small bowl, dissolve the cornstarch in the water and whisk the mixture into the fondue. When the fondue has thickened, stir in the vinegar and sesame oil.

5. Serve the fondue over medium heat. Spear and cook cubes of chicken and pork in the simmering sauce for about 2 minutes, or until cooked through. Dip the steamed bok choy into the fondue.

The Parts Equal the Whole
in Pizza Fondue

CREATE A WHOLE NEW Friday night pizza tradition, complete with sauce, dippers, and crusts. Any of your favorite pizza toppings will be at home here, along with pitchers of ice-cold beer. ● *Serves 8 (Makes 7 cups)*

FONDUE POT: Large

DIPPERS: Marinated artichoke hearts, marinated mushrooms, black olives, fresh mozzarella cubes, provolone cubes, cooked Italian fennel sausage rounds, baked pizza crust wedges

6 cups marinara sauce, homemade (page 72) or store-bought

1 cup red wine

Sea salt and freshly ground black pepper to taste

Seasonings of your choice, such as fresh basil, oregano, red pepper flakes, chopped black olives, or capers

1. Heat the marinara and wine in a large fondue pot over medium heat until the flavors combine, about 15 minutes. Taste and season with salt and pepper as needed. Stir in the additional seasonings of your choice.

2. Serve over medium-low heat.

No-Fuss Quick Marinara Sauce

● *Makes about 1⅔ cups*

2 tablespoons olive oil
1 small yellow onion, chopped
2 garlic cloves, minced
One 28-ounce can tomatoes with their juice, coarsely chopped
1½ teaspoons dried Italian seasoning, or 1 sprig each of fresh basil, thyme,
   and oregano
Sea salt and freshly ground pepper to taste

1. Heat the olive oil in a medium-size saucepan over medium heat. Stir in the onion and sauté for 3 minutes or until the onion has softened slightly. Stir in the garlic and sauté for 1 minute. Stir in the tomatoes and the Italian seasoning. Heat to a simmer, then taste and season with salt and pepper as desired.

2. Simmer for about 20 minutes, or until slightly thickened. Taste and re-season with salt and pepper if needed. The sauce is ready to use, or it can be cooled and blended in a food processor or blender into a smooth puree.

Fondue à Deux

HERE'S A FONDUE that may well lead to "I do." It's a romantic meltdown for two based on the classic red wine sauce for poached eggs. Light yet intense in color and flavor, this fondue is the way to woo a Valentine or a fiancée candidate. Thanks to cookbook author Mary Evans for the tip of adding just a pinch of Kitchen Bouquet, which keeps the color of the saucy fondue from fading. ● *Serves 2 (Makes 1½ cups)*

FONDUE POT: Small

DIPPERS: Quartered hard-boiled eggs, small toast triangles,
   seasonal vegetables

4 strips bacon, cut into ¼-inch pieces
2 chopped scallions (white and green parts)
1 cup chicken broth
1 cup red wine
½ teaspoon Kitchen Bouquet
Freshly ground black pepper to taste
3 tablespoons unsalted butter
2 tablespoons all-purpose flour
2 tablespoons minced fresh flat-leaf parsley

1. Place the bacon in a small fondue pot and cook over medium heat until crisp. Add the scallions and sauté for 2 minutes.

2. Stir in the broth, wine, and Kitchen Bouquet and season with pepper. Simmer on the lowest heat setting for 10 minutes.

3. Mix together the butter and flour in a small bowl and stir the mixture into the fondue. Cook, stirring frequently, for 3 to 5 minutes, until the fondue is thick.

4. Stir in the parsley and serve over medium-low heat.

Chorizo Cream Fondue

FIRST TASTED A VERSION of this at Pierre Gagnaire, the legendary three-star restaurant in Paris, France. It was served in a tiny porcelain cup and surrounded by lots of mysteriously flavored accompaniments. I loved it, so I scaled back the ingredients a bit to fit my budget and came up with this tasty fondue. It evokes memories of the restaurant and provides three-star flavor on a one-star budget. ● *Serves 8 (Makes 4½ cups)*

FONDUE POT: Large

DIPPERS: Sturdy vegetables such as jicama strips, green mango sticks, firm papaya slices, tortilla chips, masa rounds, chicharróns

12 ounces Mexican chorizo sausage, crumbled

One 12-ounce bottle dark Mexican beer

One 8-ounce package cream cheese, cubed

6 ounces Mexican panela cheese, cubed

2 tablespoons cornstarch

¼ cup water

½ cup medium or hot salsa

¼ cup minced fresh cilantro

1. Place the chorizo in a large fondue pot and cook over medium heat until lightly browned, about 5 minutes.

2. Reduce the heat to low and add the beer and cheeses. Cook over the lowest heat, stirring frequently, until the cheeses melt, about 10 minutes.

3. In a small bowl, dissolve the cornstarch in the water and stir the mixture into the fondue until thickened.

4. Stir in the salsa and cilantro and serve over low heat.

Pipérade Fondue

HAM AND EGGS IN A POT best describes this Basque classic turned fondue. The sauce is best when made several days ahead and reheated just before serving and adding the eggs. It's helpful to use the bread as a handheld scoop for the sauce. If you can find it, use Bayonne ham as a dipper here for the most authentic Basque flavor. ● *Serves 6 (Makes 4 cups)*

FONDUE POT: Large
DIPPERS: Thick toasted bread, cubes of cured ham

2 tablespoons olive oil
1 cup chopped yellow onion
Sea salt and freshly ground black pepper to taste
2 garlic cloves, minced
One 28-ounce can diced tomatoes with garlic and basil
1 small green bell pepper, seeded and diced
1 small red bell pepper, seeded and diced
½ cup dry red wine
2 teaspoons Italian seasoning
¼ teaspoon cayenne pepper
4 large eggs, beaten

1. Heat the oil in a large saucepan over medium heat. Add the onion, season with salt and pepper, and sauté for 5 minutes, or until the onion is browned. Stir in the garlic and cook for 20 seconds.

2. Add the tomatoes, bell peppers, wine, Italian seasoning, and cayenne. Reduce the heat to low and simmer for 30 minutes, or until the peppers are very soft.

3. Transfer the mixture to a large fondue pot and serve over medium-low heat. After dipping the bread and ham into the fondue, stir the eggs into the fondue and cook until set, about 5 minutes. Serve in bowls and provide plenty of additional toasted bread for scooping everything up.

Bourguignon Style

Bourguignon Style

Bruschetta Fondue

T'S DIFFICULT TO FIND much fresher bread than one cooked immediately before eating, as in this fondue! Be sure to pat the bread rounds into very thin silver dollar–size pancakes before frying them to ensure that they'll cook and puff thoroughly. Wait until they are slightly cool before adding the toppings and eating, as these morsels tend to hold their heat. ● *Serves 6*

FONDUE POT: Large

TOPPINGS (for the cooked bread): Assorted homemade or
store-bought pestos and bruschetta toppings, fresh mozzarella
cut into tiny pieces, shaved Parmesan, fresh arugula leaves

1 pound prepared garlic-and-herb bread dough
34 ounces canola oil

1. Break off small pieces of the dough and roll them into 1-inch balls. Arrange the dough balls on a large platter.

2. Heat the oil in a large fondue pot over medium-high heat to 350°F and maintain this heat for serving.

3. Flatten the dough balls into very flat sheets, spear with a fondue fork, and cook in the oil for 2 minutes, or until deep golden brown. Drain the cooked bread briefly on paper towels, if desired, before adding toppings.

Bagna Cauda

THE NAME OF THIS DISH, originally from the Piedmont region of Italy, translates to "hot bath." Traditionally made with both oil and butter, this version omits the butter and is just as savory. Dippers can be any seasonal fresh vegetables, breads, or crackers that appeal to your mood.

● Serves 3 or 4 as an appetizer (Makes about 1⅓ cups sauce)

FONDUE POT: Small

DIPPERS: Red bell pepper strips, lightly steamed thin asparagus spears, fennel slices, cubes of Italian bread

1¼ cups extra-virgin olive oil
4 large garlic cloves, minced
3 large salt-packed anchovies, rinsed and minced
½ small fresh serrano chile, minced
1 tablespoon minced fresh flat-leaf parsley
Sea salt and freshly ground black pepper to taste

1. Heat the olive oil, garlic, anchovies, and chile together in a small fondue pot over medium-low heat until simmering, about 3 minutes.

2. Stir in the parsley and lightly season with salt and pepper. Serve over medium-low heat.

Mini Indonesian Satay Fondue with Spicy Peanut Sauce

TEMPEH, ONE OF THE DIPPERS HERE, is a compacted block of fermented soybeans; it hails from Indonesia and is a mainstay in Bali. For a true Balinese touch, serve bowls of sticky rice to accompany the satay and peanut sauce. ● *Serves 6 (Makes 1½ cups peanut sauce)*

FONDUE POT: Large
DIPPERS: Tofu cubes (see below), tempeh cut into ½-inch cubes,
   summer squash and zucchini cut into ¾-inch cubes

One 8-ounce package extra-firm tofu
1½ quarts canola oil
2 garlic cloves, minced
1 cup coconut milk
½ cup crunchy peanut butter
2 tablespoons brown or palm sugar
1½ teaspoons dark soy sauce
½ to 1 teaspoon hot chili sauce, to your taste
1 tablespoon freshly squeezed lime juice

1. Cut the tofu into 4 slabs crosswise and lay them flat in a baking dish. Cover with plastic wrap and place a flat 1-pound weight on top of the tofu. Liquid will begin to exude from the tofu; let the tofu stand for 3 to 6 hours, then drain the liquid and cut the tofu into ¾-inch cubes.

2. Warm 1 tablespoon of the oil in a large skillet over medium heat. Sauté the garlic for 1 minute, or until lightly browned. Stir in the coconut milk, peanut butter, sugar, soy sauce, and chili sauce. Heat to a simmer.

3. Stir in the lime juice and remove the pan from the heat. Let the dipping sauce cool to room temperature.

4. Heat the remaining oil in a large fondue pot to 375°F, and maintain this heat for serving. Thread the tofu cubes and other dippers of your choice on skewers, cook them in the oil until warmed through and slightly browned, about 1 minute, then dip them in the sauce.

Tempura Fondue

PANCAKE MIX AND BEER make for an amusing East-meets-West fondue. The batter is as light as air, yet it clings to the food. The result is a perfectly tender tempura and a hit at any fondue fete. Serve this with plenty of paper towels to catch the drips. A container of pickled ginger is very refreshing to serve with this fondue (as is served with traditional tempura or sushi), and a simple side dish of fresh soybeans makes an excellent accompaniment to the tempura.

● *Serves 6 (Makes 2¼ cups batter)*

FONDUE POT: Large
DIPPERS: Asparagus tips; small mushrooms; thin celery sticks;
   baby carrots, halved lengthwise; small broccoli and cauliflower florets;
   green beans; firm tofu cubes

1¾ cups buttermilk pancake baking mix
One 12-ounce bottle lager-style beer
Tempura Dipping Sauce (page 84)
6 cups canola oil

1. Whisk together the baking mix and beer in a medium-size bowl. Bring this to the table. The batter will be bubbly and the consistency of a thin pancake batter.

2. Divide the batter among 6 small bowls and place one in front of each diner. Divide the dipping sauce among 6 small cups and place alongside the batter.

3. Heat the oil in a large fondue pot over medium heat to 375°F, and maintain this heat for serving.

4. Lightly dip the dippers of your choice in the batter and fry them for 30 to 40 seconds, or until browned. Dip into the dipping sauce.

Tempura Dipping Sauce

● *Makes about 3 cups*

2 cups Japanese dashi soup, prepared from mix
½ cup Japanese plum or rice wine
½ cup soy sauce
1 tablespoon sugar

Stir together the soup, wine, soy sauce, and sugar in a medium-size bowl.

Shrimp in Spicy Garlic Beer Fondue

NEED A YEAR-ROUND show-stopping dish that will win hearts on Super Bowl Sunday or any occasion when beer, spices, and good times are ready to roll? Stock the cooler with your favorite brew and have a bundle of napkins at the ready when serving this festive fondue. ● *Serves 4*

FONDUE POT: Large
DIPPERS: Shrimp (see below), cubes of French bread

1½ cups extra-virgin olive oil
One 12-ounce bottle mild-flavored beer
5 garlic cloves, minced
2 tablespoons freshly squeezed lemon juice
1 tablespoon Cajun spice blend
1 tablespoon soy sauce
1½ teaspoons lemon zest
3 to 5 drops hot sauce, to your taste
1 pound raw large shrimp, peeled and deveined

1. Heat the olive oil in a large fondue pot over low heat. When the oil is warm, stir in the beer, garlic, lemon juice, Cajun spice blend, soy sauce, and lemon zest. Heat to a simmer, and cook for 10 minutes over low heat. Taste the fondue and season with hot sauce.

2. Place skewers of shrimp in the fondue and cook for 3 to 4 minutes, until the shrimp are firm and cooked through. Dip the bread cubes briefly to savor the broth.

Po' Boy Fondue

EVERY ONCE IN A WHILE it's nice to enjoy a little Basin Street at home. This New Orleans classic can easily be considered authentic if served with soft little French rolls, coleslaw, and a bowl of rémoulade sauce.

Serves 4 to 6

FONDUE POT: Large
DIPPERS: Breaded oysters (see below)

¾ **cup all-purpose flour**
1 **teaspoon Cajun spice blend**
½ **teaspoon sea salt**
3 **large eggs**
½ **cup milk**
1 **cup seasoned dried bread crumbs, such as garlic-herb**
24 **oysters, shucked**
1½ **cups canola oil**
Rémoulade Sauce (recipe follows)

1. In a small bowl, stir together the flour, Cajun spice blend, and salt. In another bowl, whisk together the eggs and milk. Place the bread crumbs on a shallow plate.

2. Dredge the oysters in the flour, then coat them with the eggs and milk. Lightly coat the oysters with the bread crumbs and place them on a platter.

3. Heat the oil in a large fondue pot to 375°F and maintain this temperature for serving. Spear and fry the oysters in the oil for 2 to 2½ minutes, until browned and lightly cooked. Dip into the sauce.

Rémoulade Sauce

This sauce will keep in the refrigerator for up to 1 week.

● *Makes about ⅔ cup*

½ cup mayonnaise

2 medium-size scallions (white and green parts), minced

¼ cup minced celery

2 tablespoons tomato ketchup

1 tablespoon freshly squeezed lemon juice

2 teaspoons paprika

1 teaspoon prepared horseradish

1 teaspoon yellow mustard

Place all of the ingredients in a medium-size bowl and stir to thoroughly combine. Use immediately or cover and refrigerate.

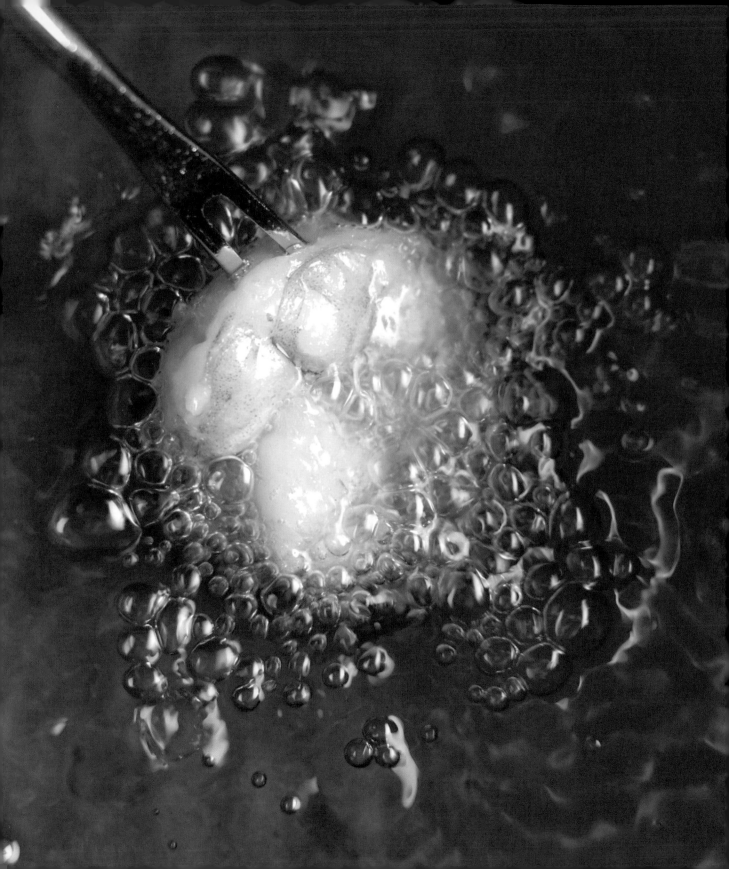

Shrimp Fondue with Senegalese Curry

THE CURRY SAUCE that goes with this fondue is thick, heady, and aromatic. You can make it several days ahead, if you like, so that the shrimp fest can be ready in just a few minutes. Serve with steamed white rice and a bottle of Asian chili-garlic sauce. ● *Serves 6 (Makes 2 cups sauce)*

FONDUE POT: Large
DIPPERS: Shrimp (see below), shrimp chips, grilled scallions,
   lightly steamed carrot sticks, raw green bell pepper strips

2 tablespoons plus 1½ quarts canola oil
2 teaspoons chili-garlic paste
3 scallions (white and green parts), chopped
2 small stalks fresh lemongrass, minced
One 13.5-ounce can coconut milk
1 tablespoon green curry paste
½ teaspoon ground turmeric
2 tablespoons minced fresh cilantro
2 tablespoons minced fresh basil
1 tablespoon cornstarch
2 tablespoons water
24 raw jumbo shrimp, peeled and deveined

1. Heat the 2 tablespoons canola oil and chili-garlic paste in a large skillet over medium heat. Stir in the scallions and lemongrass and sauté for 30 seconds. Stir in the coconut milk, curry paste, and turmeric and heat to a simmer. Cook the mixture for 10 minutes over very low heat. Stir in the cilantro and basil.

2. Dissolve the cornstarch in the water and stir the mixture into the curry sauce; cook over very low heat until thickened. Remove from the heat and let cool to room temperature before serving alongside the fondue in individual bowls or in several bowls set around the table.

3. Heat the remaining 1½ quarts canola oil in a large fondue pot to 375°F and maintain this temperature for serving. Spear and cook the shrimp for 3 to 4 minutes or until pink, firm, and cooked through. Dip the shrimp and other dippers of your choice into the curry sauce.

Tuscan Chicken Fondue

FOR THOSE WHO HAVE TRAVELED there, this fondue will bring back memories of the Chianti region of Italy, with its rustic flavors of garlic, rosemary, and basil. The simple cuisine of the area is easy to transfer to a fondue pot. Remember to remove the garlic cloves after flavoring the oil to avoid any bitterness. In addition to the Balsamic-Basil Mayonnaise, you could serve store-bought bruschetta topping or salsa verde as a dipping sauce. Serve with a side of stewed white beans, if you like. ● *Serves 6*

FONDUE POT: Large
DIPPERS: Chicken (see below), ciabatta bread or bread sticks

1½ quarts canola oil
½ cup prepared basil-flavored olive oil
4 garlic cloves
3 large sprigs fresh rosemary
1 large sprig fresh oregano
1½ pounds boneless, skinless chicken breast, cut into 1½-inch pieces
Balsamic-Basil Mayonnaise (recipe follows)

1. Place the canola oil and olive oil in a large fondue pot, and add the garlic, rosemary, and oregano. Heat the mixture to 350°F.

2. Turn off the heat and let the flavors blend for 2 to 4 hours. Remove and discard the garlic cloves.

3. When ready to serve, reheat the oil to 350°F and maintain this temperature for serving.

4. Spear the chicken pieces and cook for 4 minutes, or until firm and cooked through. Dip the chicken and other dippers of your choice into the flavored mayonnaise.

Balsamic-Basil Mayonnaise

● *Makes about 1¾ cups*

1½ cups mayonnaise
2 tablespoons balsamic vinegar
2 tablespoons minced fresh basil
1 tablespoon freshly squeezed lemon juice
2 teaspoons Dijon mustard
Sea salt and freshly ground black pepper to taste

Place the mayonnaise, vinegar, basil, lemon juice, and mustard in a large bowl and whisk until thoroughly blended and emulsified. Season with salt and pepper and refrigerate until ready to serve.

Chicken Finger Lickin' Fondue

TREAT A YOUNGER, HIP CROWD to the best chicken "fingers" they'll ever eat. The light and crunchy Japanese panko crumbs elevate chicken to a new height. Serve with good old-fashioned ketchup, the spicy ketchup from Slider Fondue with Spicy Ketchup (page 98), or the barbecue sauce from Chinese Barbecue Fondue (page 99). ● *Serves 6*

FONDUE POT: Large
DIPPER: Breaded chicken (see below)

1 cup all-purpose flour
2 teaspoons lemon pepper
3 large eggs
¾ cup milk
1½ cups panko
1½ pounds boneless, skinless chicken breast, cut into 1½-inch pieces
1½ quarts canola oil

1. Place the flour and lemon pepper in a medium-size bowl. In another smaller bowl, whisk together the eggs and milk. Place the panko on a large, shallow plate.

2. Dredge the chicken pieces in the flour mixture, then dip them into the egg mixture. Taking care to let all excess egg drip back into the bowl, dredge the chicken in the panko.

3. Heat the canola oil in a large fondue pot to 375°F and maintain this temperature for serving. Spear and cook the chicken pieces for about 4 minutes, until very brown and cooked through.

Thanksgiving Day Fondue

FOR THOSE WHO have given up having a huge traditional gathering of family and friends, this fondue is made for you. If you're planning to host just a few guests on that Thursday, try this turkey with as many trimmings as you feel like whipping up. By all means include your favorite side dishes like potatoes, wild rice, or stuffing to go with the fondue. The cranberry dip is good with any meat, both as a dip and as a glaze. It keeps well and can be frozen, so make a large batch and save some for other holiday events.

Serves 4 (Makes about 1 cup cranberry dipping sauce)

FONDUE POT: Large
DIPPER: Seasoned turkey (see below)

¾ cup jellied cranberry sauce
2 tablespoons chopped candied ginger
2 tablespoons port
1 cinnamon stick
Zest of 1 orange
2 tablespoons chopped almonds, toasted
1½ pounds boneless turkey tenderloin, cut into 1-inch cubes
2 tablespoons poultry seasoning
1½ quarts canola oil

1. Heat the cranberry sauce in a small pot on the stovetop or a large glass bowl in the microwave until it is melted and hot. Add the ginger, port, cinnamon stick, and orange zest and heat again, stirring to thoroughly combine the mixture. Stir in the almonds. Let the dipping sauce sit for at least 2 hours (at room temperature or refrigerated) before serving so that the flavors can blend.

2. Combine the turkey and poultry seasoning in a large bowl, mixing to thoroughly coat the cubes. Refrigerate, covered, for at least 1 hour before cooking.

3. Heat the oil in a large fondue pot to 375°F and maintain this temperature for serving.

4. Spear and cook the turkey cubes for 3 to 4 minutes, or until firm and thoroughly cooked. Dip the turkey into the cranberry sauce.

Middle Eastern Fondue

SERVE THIS TO A CASUAL CROWD when a roll of paper towels on the table can feel right at home. To liven up the yogurt, try sprinkling it with some cumin, paprika, and black pepper. ● *Serves 6*

FONDUE POT: Large
DIPPERS: Lamb and falafel balls (see below)

1¼ pounds lean ground lamb
1 tablespoon chopped fresh oregano
1 tablespoon chopped fresh mint, plus fresh mint sprigs for serving
2 teaspoons chopped fresh rosemary leaves
1 teaspoon ground cumin
1 teaspoon paprika
Sea salt and freshly ground black pepper to taste
One 10-ounce package falafel mix
6 cups canola oil
8 ounces thick Greek-style yogurt
One 6-ounce container prepared seasoned hummus
Pita bread wedges
Tomato wedges

1. Mix together the lamb, oregano, chopped mint, rosemary, cumin, and paprika in a medium-size bowl, and season with salt and pepper. Form the mixture into 18 balls.

2. Prepare the falafel mix according to package directions and form into 18 balls.

3. Heat the oil in a large fondue pot over medium heat to between 350° and 375°F, and maintain this temperature for serving.

4. Spear and cook the lamb and falafel balls (on separate skewers) in the hot oil for 1 to 2 minutes, or until both the lamb and falafel are browned and firm.

5. Serve along with bowls of yogurt and hummus, pita bread wedges, and tomato wedges. The mint sprigs make a refreshing palate cleanser in between bites.

Classic Beef Bourguignon Fondue

WHAT A GREAT WAY to say "Beef! It's what's for dinner!" The delicious tenderloin stands on its own in this simple but special fondue. You can be the master saucier, providing homemade or prepared dipping sauces with lots of variety and style. To elevate the dish even more, serve tiny bowls of special salts for sprinkling on the cooked beef, like French *fleur de sel*, Himalayan pink sea salt, and other specialty salts. Serve the fondue with a crisp green salad and some Burgundy. ● *Serves 6*

FONDUE POT: Large
DIPPERS: Beef pieces (see below), boiled new potatoes,
    bread cubes

4 cups canola oil
2½ pounds beef tenderloin, trimmed and cut into ¾-inch cubes
A variety of dipping sauces, such as homemade or store-bought salsas, flavored
    mayonnaises, chutneys, teriyaki sauce, Thai peanut sauce

1. Heat the oil in a large fondue pot over medium heat to 375°F and maintain this temperature for serving.

2. Spear and cook the beef in the oil for about 30 seconds for medium-rare.

3. Dip the beef and other dippers of your choice into the dipping sauces of your choice.

Chimichurri Fondue

CHIMICHURRI SAUCE is originally from Argentina, where beef reigns as king. The garlicky sauce is drizzled over grilled steaks and adored by all who love red meat. For this fondue, invite carnivores and buy the best-quality beef tenderloin you can find. Diners can cook it to their favorite "color" and dip it in the sturdy South American bath of herbs and spices.

● *Serves 6 (Makes about 1½ cups sauce)*

FONDUE POT: Large

DIPPERS: Beef pieces (see below), small baguette cubes,
    raw seasonal vegetables

⅔ **cup olive oil**
½ **cup minced fresh flat-leaf parsley**
⅓ **cup red wine vinegar**
¼ **cup minced fresh cilantro**
2 tablespoons finely minced fresh oregano
1 medium-size shallot, minced
3 garlic cloves, minced
¾ **teaspoon red pepper flakes**
Sea salt and freshly ground black pepper to taste
1½ quarts canola oil
2 pounds beef tenderloin, cut into ¾-inch cubes

1. Place the olive oil, parsley, vinegar, cilantro, oregano, shallot, garlic, and red pepper flakes in a large bowl and whisk to thoroughly blend the ingredients. Taste the chimichurri sauce and season with salt and pepper. Spoon the sauce into 6 individual small bowls.

2. Heat the oil in a large fondue pot to 375°F and maintain this temperature for serving. Spear and cook the beef in the oil for about 30 seconds for medium-rare. Dip the beef and other dippers of your choice into the bowls of chimichurri.

Slider Fondue with Spicy Ketchup

THIS FONDUE will be a definite home run for the younger set. The "sliders" here are really bun-free mini meatballs. For an older crowd, keep in mind that the sauce is also excellent with meat pâtés and scrambled eggs.

Serves 6 (Makes 2⅓ cups sauce)

FONDUE POT: Large
DIPPERS: "Sliders" (see below), French fries or
   oven-baked potato wedges

One 12-ounce jar chili sauce
1 cup ketchup
⅓ cup apple cider vinegar
¼ cup minced oil-packed sun-dried tomatoes
3 tablespoons dark brown sugar
1 tablespoon Dijon mustard
1½ quarts canola oil
1½ pounds ground beef or turkey, formed into 1-inch balls

1. Combine the chili sauce, ketchup, vinegar, sun-dried tomatoes, brown sugar, and mustard in a medium-size saucepan and heat over low heat until the mixture begins to simmer. Cook for 10 minutes, or until the sauce has thickened slightly. Transfer to a serving bowl.

2. Heat the canola oil in a large fondue pot to 375°F and maintain this temperature for serving.

3. Cook the "sliders" in the oil for 3 to 4 minutes, until firm and cooked through. Serve the spicy ketchup sauce in small individual bowls to accompany the meatballs and other dippers of your choice.

Chinese Barbecue Fondue

THIS FONDUE WILL THICKEN as it simmers, so have a small pitcher of rice wine or beer nearby to thin it as necessary. A bowl of mixed white and black sesame seeds to sprinkle on the cooked meat makes for a classy and crunchy touch. ● *Serves 6 (Makes 2 cups sauce)*

FONDUE POT: Large
DIPPERS: Duck, chicken, and pork cubes (see below)

One 18-ounce bottle smoky-sweet barbecue sauce
3 tablespoons soy sauce
1 tablespoon sesame oil
1 tablespoon minced fresh ginger
1 tablespoon hot chili-garlic paste
1½ quarts canola oil
8 ounces boneless, skinless duck breast, cut into 1-inch pieces
8 ounces boneless, skinless chicken breast, cut into 1-inch pieces
8 ounces pork tenderloin, cut into ¾-inch pieces

1. Heat the barbecue sauce, soy sauce, sesame oil, ginger, and chili-garlic paste in a saucepan over medium-low heat. Simmer for 5 minutes to combine the flavors. Let cool to room temperature before serving.

2. Heat the canola oil in a large fondue pot to 375°F and maintain this temperature for serving.

3. Skewer and cook individual cubes of the duck, chicken, and pork in the oil for about 3 minutes, until firm and cooked through. Dip into the barbecue sauce.

Charmoula Fondue

CHARMOULA IS A MOROCCAN MARINADE that contains *ras el hanout*, a mysterious spice blend that in some cases contains almost 100 different spices. Rather than make it yourself, purchase *ras el hanout* through mail-order spice companies and at better Middle Eastern groceries. A little of this exotic spice goes a long way, yet beware, because it's addicting! Before you know it, you'll be adding a pinch here and there to almost everything.

Serves 6 (Makes about 2½ cups yogurt sauce)

FONDUE POT: Large

DIPPERS: Beef, pork, or lamb pieces (see below), pita bread wedges, cherry tomatoes, cucumber spears, halved marinated artichoke hearts

1 cup olive oil

½ cup freshly squeezed lemon juice

⅓ cup chopped fresh flat-leaf parsley

⅓ cup chopped fresh cilantro

3 garlic cloves, minced

2 teaspoons lemon zest

1½ teaspoons paprika

1½ teaspoons *ras el hanout*

½ teaspoon cayenne pepper

Sea salt to taste

1½ cups plain yogurt

1½ pounds beef or pork tenderloin, or lamb loin, cut into ¾-inch cubes

One 2-ounce container prepared harissa

1½ quarts canola oil

1. In a large bowl, whisk together the oil, lemon juice, parsley, cilantro, garlic, lemon zest, paprika, *ras el hanout*, and cayenne. Taste and season with salt. Transfer 1 cup of the charmoula mixture to a separate bowl, add the yogurt, stir to combine, then cover and refrigerate until ready to serve.

2. Add the meat cubes to the remaining charmoula mixture, and stir to coat the meat. Cover and refrigerate for at least 2 hours or up to 24 hours. Bring to room temperature before serving.

3. Heat the oil in a large fondue pot to 375°F and maintain this temperature for serving. Cook the meat cubes in the oil for about 3 minutes, or until cooked through. Dip the cooked meat and other dippers of your choice into the yogurt-charmoula sauce. Serve the harissa in a small bowl to dab on the meat or top the yogurt.

New Orleans Sausage Fondue

N OWADAYS THERE ARE SO MANY creative ways to eat sausage. Try using spicy chicken with sun-dried tomato sausage, or turkey-apple sausage, or exotically spiced pork sausage for this simple fondue that is perfect to serve at a cocktail party or casual supper. Serve with a variety of hot sauces, along with my neighbor Miss Lee's famous Cajun sauce. ● *Serves 4*

FONDUE POT: Large
DIPPERS: Sausage rounds (see below)

1½ quarts canola oil
1 pound cooked spicy chicken or turkey sausage, cut into ¼-inch rounds
8 ounces cooked andouille sausage, cut into ¼-inch rounds
Miss Lee's Cajun Sauce (recipe follows)
Mini biscuits

1. Heat the oil in a large fondue pot to 375°F and maintain this temperature for serving.

2. Spear and cook the sausage rounds in the oil for 1 minute or until heated through. Dip into the Cajun sauce and serve with mini biscuits.

Miss Lee's Cajun Sauce

● *Makes about 2 cups*

1½ cups sour cream
¼ cup freshly squeezed lemon juice
2 tablespoons Creole mustard
1 tablespoon Cajun spice blend
Sea salt and freshly ground black pepper to taste

Mix together the sour cream, lemon juice, mustard, and Cajun spice blend in a small bowl. As different Cajun spice blends may vary in salt and heat, taste before seasoning with salt and pepper.

Minnesota Corn Dogs on a Stick Fondue

STATE FAIRS, LIKE CIRCUSES, are the best excuse to indulge in treats that are fun, slightly naughty, and delightfully delicious. At the Minnesota State Fair in St. Paul, happy kids form long lines to buy corn dogs, which they dip into ballpark mustard, sweet relish, and ketchup. You can buy fancy sausages or stick to standard cocktail franks or precooked sausages of any type. Make sure to be generous with the dredging step, so that the batter will adhere to the sausages and won't end up dripping into the oil. ● *Serves 6*

FONDUE POT: Large
DIPPERS: Corn dogs (see below)

¾ cup yellow cornmeal
¾ cup all-purpose flour
1 teaspoon baking powder
1 teaspoon sea salt
½ teaspoon baking soda
Pinch of cayenne pepper
1 cup plain yogurt or buttermilk
One 8-ounce can creamed corn
One 14-ounce package small cocktail franks (about 30) or any
    precooked sausage links, cut into 1-inch pieces
½ cup cornstarch
1 quart canola oil
Marinara sauce, chili sauce, and/or homemade or
    prepared cocktail relish for serving

1. Stir together the cornmeal, flour, baking powder, salt, baking soda, and cayenne in a large bowl. Stir in the yogurt and corn and mix until the ingredients are just combined to form a thick and slightly lumpy batter.

2. Dredge the sausages in the cornstarch, then dip them into the batter to thoroughly coat them. The sausages can be left to soak in the batter for up to 15 minutes before cooking.

3. Heat the canola oil in a large fondue pot to 375°F and maintain this temperature for serving.

4. Spear the sausages, allowing excess batter to drip back into the bowl. Cook in the oil until browned and slightly puffy, 3 to 4 minutes. Drain on paper towels and cool slightly before dipping in the sauce of your choice and eating.

Shades of Shabu-Shabu

Shades of Shabu-Shabu

French Onion Soup Fondue

THIS BRASSERIE CLASSIC can be transferred easily to a fondue pot. The flavor will take you right to the heart of Les Halles in Paris. Have soup bowls ready so that you can ladle the rest of the broth into them to eat after the bread is gone. ● *Serves 6 (Makes about 4 cups)*

FONDUE POT: Large

DIPPERS: Bread rounds sprinkled with Gruyère cheese and toasted; plain toasted bread; untoasted baguette cubes

3 tablespoons unsalted butter

2 medium-size Walla Walla or other sweet onions, thinly sliced

2 teaspoons sugar

Sea salt and freshly ground black pepper to taste

2 cups white wine

1 bay leaf

1 teaspoon dried thyme

3 cups chicken or beef broth

2 tablespoons cornstarch

¼ cup water or additional wine

1. Heat the butter in a large fondue pot over medium-low heat. Sauté the onions in the butter for 3 minutes. Stir in the sugar and season generously with salt and pepper. Cook for another 2 minutes.

2. Add the wine, bay leaf, and thyme and heat to a simmer. Reduce the heat to very low and cook for 50 minutes to 1 hour, or until almost all of the wine has evaporated and the onions are tender.

3. Stir in the broth and bring to a simmer over medium heat. Dissolve the cornstarch in the water and whisk the mixture into the broth until the fondue has slightly thickened.

4. Serve on the lowest heat setting.

Potato-Leek Brothy Fondue

THIS FONDUE IS A VEGETARIAN'S PARADISE. Depending on your crowd's preference, use either regular milk or soy milk. Hope that you'll have leftovers, because they make for a delicious cuppa soup with a sandwich lunch. ● *Serves 6 (Makes 5 cups)*

FONDUE POT: Large
DIPPERS: Assorted breads and crackers, seasonal vegetables, tofu triangles

3 cups vegetable broth
2 large red potatoes (about 1 pound), scrubbed and cut into 1-inch cubes
2 leeks, cleaned and chopped
3 garlic cloves, halved
½ cup milk or soy milk
Sea salt and freshly ground black pepper to taste
2 scallions (white and green parts), chopped

1. Place the broth, potatoes, leeks, and garlic in a medium-size saucepan and bring to a boil over medium heat. Reduce the heat and simmer for 20 to 25 minutes, or until the potatoes are very tender.

2. Let the mixture cool and then place in a blender. Blend into a smooth and creamy puree. Transfer to a large fondue pot.

3. Add the milk to the pot. Taste and season generously with salt and pepper. Stir in the scallions and serve over low heat.

Curried Calamari Fondue

HERE'S A FONDUE that is excellent when served as the main event of an Indian feast for friends. Serve a variety of Indian chutneys and pickles alongside the fondue. The quick sauce of curry mayonnaise is a simple and excellent accompaniment. If you use whole baby squid, ask the fishmonger for the bodies only, as the tentacles are tricky to keep on the skewers.

● *Serves 4 (Makes about 7 cups)*

FONDUE POT: Large

DIPPERS: Squid (see below), cooked cubes of white and sweet potato, cooked cauliflower florets, Indian poppadums

8 curry-flavored wooden skewers (page 8)

1 cup white wine

Two 5-ounce squid steaks, cut into 2 x 16½-inch strips, or
    10 ounces baby squid, cut into rings

6 cups chicken or vegetable broth

2 garlic cloves, minced

1 tablespoon minced fresh ginger

¾ cup mayonnaise mixed with 2 teaspoons curry powder, for serving

1. Using a shallow pan, soak the skewers in the wine for 30 minutes.

2. Thread 2 squid strips onto each of the skewers, forming two U-shaped strips on each.

3. Add the wine used for soaking the skewers to a large fondue pot along with the broth, garlic, and ginger. Heat over medium heat until simmering, about 5 minutes, then continue to cook for 10 minutes. Maintain at a simmer for serving.

4. Cook the skewers in the fondue for 1 minute, or until the squid is just firm. Heat any vegetable dippers you are serving in the fondue. Dip the cooked squid and vegetables and the poppadums into the curried mayo.

Provençal Fish Fondue with Saffron

THIS CLASSIC PROVENÇAL MEAL in a bowl adapts beautifully for a fondue fete. Any leftover fish can be simmered in the remaining reduced broth, for a sensational pasta sauce. The rouille keeps for several days, so it can be made ahead if you wish. ● *Serves 6 (Makes about 5¼ cups)*

FONDUE POT: Large
DIPPERS: Assorted seafood (see below), French bread cubes

1 tablespoon olive oil
2 shallots, minced
2 garlic cloves, minced
One 28-ounce can diced tomatoes
1½ cups vegetable broth
½ cup red wine
1½ teaspoons anchovy paste
½ teaspoon saffron
Large pinch of cayenne pepper
Zest of 1 orange
Sea salt and freshly ground black pepper to taste
8 ounces raw large shrimp, peeled and deveined
8 ounces salmon fillet, cut into ¾-inch cubes
8 ounces firm white fish, such as halibut, sea bass, or cod, cut into ¾-inch cubes
12 large scallops
Quick Rouille (recipe follows)

1. Heat the oil in a large fondue pot over medium heat. Add the shallots and sauté in the oil for 2 minutes, until softened. Stir in the garlic and sauté for 30 seconds.

2. Stir in the tomatoes, broth, wine, anchovy paste, saffron, cayenne, and orange zest. Season with salt and pepper. Simmer the mixture for 20 minutes.

3. Serve the fondue over medium-low heat. Spear individual cubes of the seafood and cook until done, about 2½ minutes. Dip into the rouille. The bread is good dipped in the "bouillabaisse" or just munched on between fish bites.

Quick Rouille

● *Makes about 1 cup*

¼ teaspoon saffron
2 tablespoons warm water
1 cup mayonnaise
2 large garlic cloves, minced
4 drops to ½ teaspoon hot sauce, to your taste
Sea salt and freshly ground black pepper

Dissolve the saffron in the warm water in a small bowl. Add the mayonnaise and whisk to blend. Stir in the garlic and hot sauce and season with salt and pepper. Refrigerate until ready to serve.

O Sole Mio Brochettes Fondue

REINFORCE THE ITALIAN THEME here by serving a tray of assorted antipasti and a bottle of Prosecco along with the fondue. Feel free to substitute any fresh flatfish for the sole, such as tilapia.

● *Serves 6 (Makes 5 cups)*

FONDUE POT: Large
DIPPERS: Fish strips and potato cubes (see below)

1½ pounds sole fillets, cut into 1 x 2-inch strips
1 tablespoon lemon pepper
1 pound mixed yellow, red, and purple potatoes, scrubbed
5 cups fish or vegetable broth
1 large shallot, minced
1 garlic clove, minced
1 teaspoon dried Italian seasoning
Dipping sauces of your choice for serving, such as sour cream or yogurt flavored with different store-bought pestos; store-bought bruschetta topping; store-bought or homemade olivada (page 32)

1. Lightly season the fish with the lemon pepper and fold each strip into thirds, to make folded squares. Place on a platter. Cut the potatoes into small cubes and cook in salted water until tender, 10 to 12 minutes. Drain and place in a serving bowl.

2. Place the broth in a large fondue pot along with the shallot, garlic, and Italian seasoning. Heat to a simmer over medium heat and cook for 10 minutes. Maintain at a simmer for serving.

3. Spear the fish and cook it in the simmering fondue for 1 minute, or until firm. Warm the potatoes in the fondue. Serve the fish and potatoes with the dipping sauces of your choice.

Lemongrass Broth for Shrimp and Scallop Fondue

GALANGAL IS A RHIZOME, like ginger, that can be found in many Asian markets carrying Indonesian and Malaysian supplies. There you'll also find *kecap manis*, a thick, hot, and sweet sauce. Other Asian hot sauces may be substituted for the *kecap manis*, with a very tasty if slightly less authentic result. ● *Serves 6 (Makes 4½ cups broth)*

FONDUE POT: Large

DIPPERS: Scallops and shrimp (see below), snow peas,
   baby bok choy leaves

4 cups fish or vegetable broth
2 large stalks lemongrass, cut into 2-inch pieces, or
   1 tablespoon dried lemongrass
3 garlic cloves, crushed
3 scallions (white and green parts), cut into 2-inch pieces
1 tablespoon minced fresh ginger
2 teaspoons minced fresh galangal
1 tablespoon *kecap manis* or hot chili sauce
1 tablespoon minced fresh basil
1 tablespoon minced fresh mint
Sea salt to taste
1½ pounds large shrimp, peeled and deveined
1½ pounds small scallops

1. Heat the broth, lemongrass, garlic, scallions, ginger, and galangal in a large fondue pot over medium heat. When the broth begins to simmer, reduce the heat to medium-low and cook for 10 minutes. Maintain at a simmer for serving.

2. Stir in the *kecap manis*, basil, and mint. Season with salt.

3. Spear and cook the shrimp and scallops in the simmering fondue for 3 to 4 minutes, or until firm and cooked through. Dip the snow peas and baby bok choy leaves briefly in the broth to warm and flavor them.

Southern-Style Catfish Fondue

OUR SOUTHERN STATES have a tradition of poaching fish, particularly catfish, in milk, which is similar to the Italian technique of cooking pork in milk. It makes for a great fondue, too. You'll be amazed at the moist texture of the fish. ● *Serves 4 (Makes about 3½ cups)*

FONDUE POT: Medium
DIPPERS: Fish cubes (see below)

1½ cups milk
1 cup fish or vegetable broth
1 cup dry white wine
Zest of 1 lemon
1 bay leaf
1 teaspoon dried dill weed
1 tablespoon cornstarch
2 tablespoons water
1 pound catfish or other thick white fish fillets, cut into 1-inch cubes
Rémoulade Sauce (page 87) or ⅔ cup tartar sauce, for serving

1. Heat the milk, broth, wine, lemon zest, bay leaf, and dill weed in a medium-size fondue pot over medium-low heat. When the fondue begins to simmer, reduce the heat to low and cook for 5 minutes. Maintain at a simmer for serving.

2. Dissolve the cornstarch in the water and whisk the mixture into the fondue, stirring until the fondue is smooth and slightly thickened.

3. Spear and cook the fish in the simmering fondue for about 1½ minutes, or until firm and cooked through. Dip the fish into the rémoulade.

Spring Roll "Fondue"

BASED ON A TECHNIQUE I first spied in tiny Kim's Asian Café in Encinitas, California, the broth used here is just plain ol' hot water! Use this "fondue" for softening the rice papers. Once they are malleable, wrap them around the grilled shrimp, crunchy sprouts, nuts, and cilantro, along with any cooked Asian vegetables that strike your fancy. One can eat this dish for hours and hours! Plain steamed shrimp are fine for this fondue if grilling is inconvenient. ● *Serves 4*

FONDUE POT: Large

1½ quarts water
12 ounces raw jumbo shrimp, peeled and deveined
½ cup rice wine
¼ cup prepared Thai or Indonesian peanut sauce
One 8-ounce package bean sprouts
1 small bunch fresh cilantro, coarsely chopped
¼ cup finely chopped salted roasted peanuts
Hot chili sauce
One 12-ounce package Thai-style rice papers

1. Add the water to a large fondue pot and heat to a boil.

2. Mix together the shrimp, rice wine, and peanut sauce in a medium-size bowl and let marinate in the refrigerator for 30 minutes. Heat a charcoal or gas grill or a grill pan on the stovetop and cook the shrimp for 3 to 5 minutes, until firm and pink.

3. Place the bean sprouts, cilantro, and peanuts on a platter, then place the platter and a bottle of hot chili sauce on the serving table. Soften the rice papers in the water for about 45 seconds, then remove them with fondue forks. Place the softened rice papers on paper towels to blot dry, then transfer them to individual serving plates. Make spring rolls by filling the rice papers with the warm shrimp, bean sprouts, cilantro, and peanuts; adding hot chili sauce; and rolling them up.

Miso Fondue with Fish and Shiitake Mushrooms

I F YOU'RE LOOKING for a tasty, low-fat, low-calorie meal for entertaining, read on! This variation on an Asian hot pot can be dressed up or down as your budget permits. Try a variety of fish, shellfish, and wild mushrooms. All lend themselves beautifully to this simple and light broth, which will get richer and even more savory as the evening goes by. Serve steamed rice alongside so you can pour the leftover broth over it. ● *Serves 3 to 4 (Makes about 8½ cups broth)*

FONDUE POT: Large
DIPPERS: Fish cubes and mushroom pieces (see below),
celery sticks, baked tofu cubes

8 cups vegetable broth
10 ounces shredded cabbage (about 8½ cups)
4 strips dried kombu seaweed, soaked and cut into 1-inch pieces (about ¼ cup)
1 tablespoon minced garlic
1 tablespoon white miso
1 pound halibut, skinned and cut into 1-inch cubes
4 ounces fresh shiitake mushrooms, stemmed and halved

1. Heat the broth, cabbage, seaweed, garlic, and miso in a large fondue pot over low heat for 15 minutes. Maintain at a simmer for serving.

2. Spear and cook the fish and mushrooms in the simmering broth for about 1 minute, or until firm and warm. Dip the celery sticks and baked tofu cubes in the broth to warm and flavor them.

Mongolian Hot Pot

MIX AND MATCH is the name of the game for this fondue. Try any leafy vegetable for dipping into the broth, and serve a variety of dipping sauces alongside. This is truly a feast of flavors that can be custom-designed to the diner. Any type of whitefish such as snapper, cod, or halibut can be used. ● *Serves 6 (Makes about 5 cups)*

FONDUE POT: Large
DIPPERS: Fish cubes and shrimp (see below), Chinese cabbage leaves,
　　spinach leaves

4 cups chicken or fish broth

1 cup water

2 tablespoons rice vinegar

One 2-inch piece fresh ginger, crushed

4 scallions (white and green parts), cut into 2-inch pieces

½ teaspoon red pepper flakes

12 ounces whitefish fillets, cut into 1-inch cubes

12 ounces raw large shrimp, peeled and deveined

**Dipping sauces of your choice, such as light or dark soy sauce, plum sauce, hoisin
　　sauce, miso**

1. Place the broth, water, rice vinegar, ginger, scallions, and red pepper flakes in a large fondue pot and bring to a simmer. Simmer for 5 minutes.

2. Keep the simmering broth on the low heat setting. Spear the seafood and vegetables and cook them in the fondue for 1 to 2 minutes, until the seafood is firm and the vegetables have wilted slightly. Dip into the dipping sauce of your choice.

Saffron Broth Fondue

DEPENDING ON THE POTENCY of your saffron, the amount needed for this fondue will vary. Whatever quantity you use, soften the saffron in milk as directed in step 1. The Indian kitchen guru Madhur Jaffrey taught this technique to me in the 1990s, and I have religiously followed her advice ever since. ● *Serves 6 (Makes about 5 cups)*

FONDUE POT: Large
DIPPERS: Fish cubes (see below), French bread cubes, seasonal vegetables

½ teaspoon saffron
1 tablespoon milk
2 tablespoons olive oil
1 small yellow onion, chopped
2 garlic cloves, chopped
1 tablespoon fennel seed
2 teaspoons pink peppercorns
1 teaspoon celery seed
4 cups vegetable or fish broth
1 cup dry white wine
Sea salt and freshly ground black pepper to taste
2½ pounds assorted firm fish, such as tilapia, flounder, bass, or swordfish, cut into 1-inch cubes

1. In a small cup, soften the saffron in the milk.

2. Heat the oil in a large fondue pot over low heat. Add the onion, garlic, fennel seed, peppercorns, and celery seed. Sauté for 3 minutes.

3. Stir in the broth, wine, and softened saffron and heat to a simmer. Cook at a simmer for 10 minutes. Season with salt and pepper. Maintain at a simmer for serving.

4. Dip and cook the fish cubes in the simmering broth for 2 minutes, or until firm. Dip the bread and vegetables lightly; the bread will soak up the broth, and the vegetables will soften and become more flavorful.

Shrimp Bisque Fondue

YOU ARE ONLY 30 MINUTES AWAY from luxury with this broth, and the secret is a can of all-American tomato soup! This fondue wins the hearts of shrimp lovers and true gourmands. In other words, a little will scarcely be enough, so feel free to double the recipe. ● *Serves 6 (Makes about 5 cups)*

FONDUE POT: Large
DIPPERS: Shrimp (see below), cubes of warm garlic bread,
celery stalks, fennel slices, and other firm raw vegetables

2 pounds raw large shrimp, peeled and deveined
3 tablespoons unsalted butter
2 large shallots, minced
4½ teaspoons all-purpose flour
2½ cups chicken broth
One 10.75-ounce can condensed tomato soup
1 cup heavy cream
⅔ cup dry sherry
1 tablespoon minced fresh dill

1. Finely chop 8 ounces of the shrimp and set aside.

2. Melt the butter in a large fondue pot over medium-low heat. Add the shallots and sauté for 3 minutes. Stir in the flour and cook for 3 minutes.

3. Stir in the chopped shrimp, broth, and soup and heat to a simmer. Stir in the cream and sherry and sprinkle the dill on top. Keep at a simmer for serving.

4. Spear one or two shrimp at a time and cook in the simmering broth for 3 to 4 minutes, or until firm, pink, and cooked through. Briefly dip the bread and vegetables to absorb the broth.

Pungent Carrot-Ginger Fondue

T HIS FONDUE IS A SNAP TO MAKE in a food processor. The finished broth will please any vegan palate, as well as poultry and fish lovers. Vary the dippers according to your crowd's tastes. ● *Serves 6 (Makes about 4 cups)*

FONDUE POT: Large

DIPPERS: Cubes of tofu, tempeh, whitefish, and/or chicken (see below); snow peas; bell pepper strips

1½ cups peeled and sliced carrots

2⅔ cups vegetable or chicken broth

1 medium-size yellow onion, chopped (about ¾ cup)

4½ teaspoons chopped fresh ginger

1¾ cups California Gewürztraminer or other fruity white wine

½ cup orange juice

2 tablespoons minced fresh chives

Sea salt and freshly ground black pepper to taste

8 ounces extra-firm tofu, cut into ½-inch cubes

One 8-ounce package tempeh, cut into ½-inch cubes

8 ounces boneless, skinless chicken breast, cut into 1-inch cubes

8 ounces whitefish fillets, cut into 1-inch pieces

1. Place the carrots and ¾ cup of the broth in a food processor and pulse to finely mince the carrots.

2. Place the onion, ginger, and ¾ cup of the wine in a large fondue pot and bring to a simmer over low heat. Cook for 5 to 7 minutes, or until the wine has evaporated.

3. Stir in the carrot broth along with the remaining vegetable broth and remaining 1 cup wine. Simmer for 20 to 25 minutes, or until the carrots are almost tender. Stir in the orange juice and chives. Taste and season with salt and pepper. Maintain at a simmer for serving.

4. Spear the tofu, tempeh, chicken, and fish and cook in the simmering broth until the chicken and fish are firm (about 3 minutes for the chicken and fish; the tofu and tempeh will just need to be heated in the broth). Lightly dip the vegetables to flavor and soften slightly.

Tomatillo Broth Fondue

BASED ON THE MEXICAN TECHNIQUE of preparing soups and sauces by sautéing them first and then pureeing them in a blender, this fondue incorporates tomatillos and south-of-the-border spices. In addition to the dippers, serve cubes of jicama and tropical fruits on the platter as well as a big bowl of homemade or prepared salsa. *Arepas* are a kind of South American cornbread. ● *Serves 6 (Makes 4 cups)*

FONDUE POT: Large
DIPPERS: Pork and/or chicken cubes (see below)

2 tablespoons canola oil
1 medium-size white onion, coarsely chopped
2 garlic cloves, halved
¾ teaspoon ground cumin
1 fresh serrano chile, seeded and minced
One 28-ounce can tomatillos, drained (10 tomatillos)
2 cups chicken broth
2 tablespoons minced fresh cilantro
Sea salt and freshly ground black pepper to taste
1½ pounds pork or chicken, cut into 1-inch cubes
Tortilla chips
Arepas wedges

1. Heat the oil in a medium-size skillet over medium heat. Sauté the onion, garlic, cumin, and chile until the onion has softened, about 3 minutes. Stir in the tomatillos and heat the mixture to a simmer, breaking up the tomatillos with a spoon.

2. Simmer over low heat for 3 minutes, then carefully transfer the mixture to a blender. Blend into a smooth puree and pour into a large fondue pot.

3. Stir in the broth and cilantro and heat the fondue to a simmer, 5 to 8 minutes. Season with salt and pepper and serve over low heat. Skewer the pork or chicken cubes and cook in the hot broth for 3 to 4 minutes, until firm and cooked through.

Panang Curry Fondue

YOUR LOCAL ASIAN MARKET is sure to carry a variety of curry pastes. Almost any will work well in this easy-to-prepare fondue. Once everything is in the pot and thickened, thin the broth as necessary with additional coconut milk or beer. ● *Serves 4 (Makes 3 cups)*

FONDUE POT: Medium

DIPPERS: Cooked chicken or fish cubes, radishes, snow peas, lightly steamed scallions, wedges of fruits such as pineapple, mango, papaya, Asian pear, and starfruit

One 13.5-ounce can coconut milk
8 ounces Thai beer
⅓ cup unsweetened shredded coconut
3 tablespoons Panang curry paste
¼ cup chopped fresh cilantro

1. Heat the coconut milk, beer, shredded coconut, and curry paste in a medium-size fondue pot over medium-low heat for about 10 minutes. When the mixture simmers, stir in the cilantro.

2. Serve over low heat.

Coq au Vin Fondue

FRANCOPHILES AND WINE LOVERS alike will appreciate this quick take on the classic long-simmered stew. Serve a solid Côtes du Rhône wine along with it, and toast as well as taste *la belle France*.

● *Serves 4 (Makes about 5½ cups)*

FONDUE POT: Large
DIPPERS: Pearl onions, mushrooms, chicken (see below)

3 strips smoked bacon, chopped
1 tablespoon all-purpose flour
4 cups chicken broth
1 cup red wine
½ cup prepared marinara sauce
2 garlic cloves, minced
1 teaspoon dried *herbes de Provence*
Sea salt and freshly ground black pepper to taste
1 pound pearl onions, thawed if frozen
8 ounces cremini mushrooms, halved
1½ pounds boneless, skinless chicken breast, cut into ¾-inch pieces

1. Place the bacon in a large fondue pot and cook over medium heat until browned. Stir in the flour and cook for 2 minutes.

2. Stir in the broth, wine, marinara, garlic, and *herbes de Provence* and heat to a simmer. Season with salt and pepper. Maintain at a simmer for serving.

3. Spear the onions and mushrooms and cook in the fondue for 1 to 2 minutes, or until heated through. Spear the chicken and cook in the fondue for 3 to 4 minutes, or until firm and cooked through.

Thai Tom Yum Chicken Fondue

THE CLASSIC THAI SOUP is an excellent broth for fondue. With the rice noodles, this fondue becomes a meal in itself. Serve the warm spiced broth and noodles in colorful bowls. A medium-dry white wine is an excellent accompaniment. ● *Serves 6 (Makes about 8¼ cups)*

FONDUE POT: Large
DIPPERS: Chicken cubes and mushrooms (see below)

8 cups fish or vegetable broth
1 large stalk fresh lemongrass
3 tablespoons freshly squeezed lime juice
2 tablespoons Thai fish sauce
4 fresh or dried kaffir lime leaves (optional)
3 to 6 fresh jalapeño or serrano chiles, to your taste, halved and seeded
2 pounds boneless, skinless chicken breast, cut into 1-inch cubes
1½ pounds small cremini mushrooms, halved
1 pound fresh rice noodles
1 large bunch fresh cilantro sprigs

1. Place the broth, lemongrass, lime juice, fish sauce, lime leaves (if using), and chiles in a large fondue pot and bring to a simmer over medium heat. Cook for 5 minutes. Maintain at a simmer for serving.

2. Skewer cubes of chicken and mushrooms together and cook in the simmering broth for 3 to 4 minutes, or until the chicken is white and firm.

3. After diners have finished cooking the chicken and mushrooms, place the rice noodles in the broth and cook until heated through, about 3 minutes. Serve small bowls of the noodles with some broth poured over the top, garnished with cilantro sprigs.

Wild Mushroom and Sherry Fondue

TUCKED AWAY IN A SMALL CORNER of La Boqueria—the covered market in Barcelona, Spain—is a charming family-run café that serves daily specials based on whatever the neighboring food stalls are selling. In September, there is usually a soup like this broth, filled with wild mushrooms and heady with sherry. Diners order it with either chicken or pork. As you'll taste, this Catalonian memory translates beautifully into fondue.

● *Serves 6 (Makes 5 cups)*

FONDUE POT: Large
DIPPERS: Chicken or pork cubes (see below),
small mushrooms

½ ounce dried shiitake mushrooms (6 mushrooms)
2 cups warm water
2 shallots, minced
2 garlic cloves, chopped
1 tablespoon olive oil
2 ounces pancetta, chopped
4 cups chicken broth
½ cup dry Spanish sherry
¼ cup heavy cream
1 tablespoon minced fresh flat-leaf parsley
1 tablespoon minced fresh basil
Sea salt and freshly ground black pepper to taste
1½ pounds boneless, skinless chicken breast or
pork tenderloin, cut into 1-inch cubes

1. In a small bowl, soak the mushrooms in the warm water for at least 1 hour or until soft. Drain, reserving the liquid. Stem and chop the mushrooms and set aside.

2. Place the shallots, garlic, oil, and pancetta in a large fondue pot over medium-low heat. Sauté until the pancetta is slightly crisp.

3. Stir in the mushrooms, reserved soaking liquid, and the broth. Simmer for 15 minutes.

4. Stir in the sherry, cream, parsley, and basil and simmer for 5 minutes. Season with salt and pepper. Maintain at a simmer for serving.

5. Spear pork or chicken cubes and cook for 3 to 4 minutes in the simmering broth, or until firm and cooked through. Spear the mushrooms and cook in the broth until heated through and slightly softened.

Chinese Master Sauce Fondue

MASTER SAUCE is extremely revered in Chinese households. The sauce is kept and constantly added to for years. Rock sugar is traditionally used to produce the balanced sweet-and-salty flavor, along with soy sauce. Asian markets usually stock amber-colored rock sugar; however, feel free to substitute brown sugar. ● *Serves 6 (Makes about 4 cups)*

FONDUE POT: Large
DIPPERS: Chicken cubes (see below), firm tofu cubes, small steamed Chinese dumplings, seasonal Asian vegetables, cooked noodles

¾ **cup dark soy sauce**
¾ **cup light soy sauce**
¾ **cup rice wine**
2 **tablespoons rock sugar or dark brown sugar**
1 **tablespoon granulated sugar**
1 **tablespoon minced fresh ginger**
2 **cups chicken broth**
Zest of 1 orange, minced
2 **garlic cloves, crushed**
2 **scallions (white and green parts), cut into 2-inch pieces**
1 **teaspoon crushed Sichuan peppercorns**
2 **teaspoons toasted sesame oil**
18 **ounces boneless, skinless chicken breast, cut into 1-inch pieces**

1. Place the soy sauces, rice wine, sugars, and ginger in a large fondue pot and heat to a simmer. Cook for 5 minutes.

2. Stir in the chicken broth, orange zest, garlic, scallions, and peppercorns. Reheat to a simmer and cook for an additional 5 minutes. Stir in the oil. Maintain at a simmer for serving.

3. Spear and cook the chicken cubes in the simmering broth for about 3 minutes, or until firm and cooked through. Dip the tofu, dumplings, and vegetables in the broth to flavor and warm them. After the dippers have been eaten, place the noodles in small bowls and pour the remaining broth over them.

French Dip Fondue

THE ALWAYS-PRESENT LUNCH SPECIAL at my favorite steakhouse provided the inspiration for this nifty crowd-pleaser. Use plain beef broth, or spice it up first with garlic, parsley, and cayenne pepper. Feel free to substitute turkey, pastrami, or other deli meats for the roast beef. Serve with side dishes of coleslaw, potato salad, and pickles. ● *Serves 6 (Makes 7 cups)*

FONDUE POT: Large
DIPPERS: Roast beef chunks (see below), mini bagels or soft rolls (see below), cherry tomatoes or thickly sliced tomatoes

7 cups beef broth
2 cups sour cream
½ cup prepared horseradish
Sea salt to taste
12 ounces rare roast beef, cut into chunks
Twelve 1-ounce soft rolls or mini bagels

1. Heat the broth in a large fondue pot over medium heat. As the broth warms, mix together the sour cream and horseradish in a medium-size bowl and season with salt.

2. Serve the fondue over medium-low heat. Dip the roast beef chunks and bread in the broth, then dip in the horseradish sauce. The tomatoes can be served alongside or also lightly dipped in the broth to flavor them.

Ginger Beef Fondue

FRAGRANT BEEFY BROTH is an easy and effortless way to cook steak. Be sure to serve a big bowl of prepared bean thread noodles alongside the fondue, so that you can pour the last of the broth over the noodles.

Serves 6 (Makes 4 cups)

FONDUE POT: Large

DIPPERS: Steak cubes (see below), lightly steamed broccoli florets, baby bok choy leaves, Chinese cabbage leaves

4 cups beef broth

2 tablespoons soy sauce

2 tablespoons balsamic vinegar

1 tablespoon minced fresh ginger

1 tablespoon dark brown sugar

1 teaspoon chile-flavored sesame oil

2 garlic cloves, bruised (not crushed)

3 scallions (white and green parts), coarsely chopped

2 pounds tender steak filet, such as beef tenderloin, cut into ¾-inch cubes

1. Combine the broth, soy sauce, vinegar, ginger, brown sugar, sesame oil, and garlic in a large fondue pot over medium heat.

2. When the mixture reaches a simmer, stir in the scallions. Maintain at a simmer for serving.

3. Skewer and cook the steak cubes in the simmering broth until just firm and done to taste, about 30 seconds for medium-rare. Dip the vegetables in the broth to soften and flavor them.

Mega Garlic Broth Fondue

SERVE SLABS OF TOASTED COUNTRY BREAD toward the end of the meal to smear with the delectably soft garlic cloves. ● *Serves 6 (Makes 4 cups)*

FONDUE POT: Large
DIPPERS: Pork or chicken cubes (see below),
    just about any seasonal vegetable

2 large heads garlic, separated into unpeeled cloves (about 20 cloves)
4 cups vegetable or chicken broth
1 bay leaf
Pinch of cayenne pepper
¼ cup fresh basil leaves, cut into julienne strips
1½ pounds pork tenderloin or boneless, skinless chicken breast,
    cut into ¾-inch cubes

1. Preheat the oven to 375°F. Wrap the garlic in aluminum foil and roast for 30 minutes. Remove from the foil.

2. Place the garlic cloves, broth, bay leaf, and cayenne in a large fondue pot and heat over medium heat until the broth simmers. Simmer on the lowest possible setting for 20 minutes or until the garlic cloves are very soft. Maintain at a simmer for serving.

3. Sprinkle the fondue with the basil. Skewer and cook the pork or chicken in the simmering broth for 3 to 4 minutes, or until firm. Dip the vegetables in the broth to flavor and slightly soften them. If desired, diners may fish out the garlic cloves, squeeze them from their skins, and devour.

Madeira Fondue for Ham

CLASSIC MADEIRA SAUCE, traditionally served with ham or beef, makes a wonderful base for an elegant holiday fondue. Prepare an easy dipping sauce of sour cream mixed with horseradish to serve with the ham, and round out the festive meal with a tray of mini popovers.

● *Serves 6 (Makes about 5 cups)*

FONDUE POT: Large
DIPPERS: Ham cubes (see below)

2 cups beef broth
1¼ cups dry red wine
2 garlic cloves, minced
1 tablespoon cornstarch
1⅔ cups Madeira
2 tablespoons unsalted butter
One 3-inch sprig fresh thyme
One 3-inch sprig fresh rosemary
1 bay leaf
Sea salt and freshly ground black pepper to taste
1½ pounds cured ham, cut into bite-size cubes

1. Place the beef broth, red wine, and garlic in a large fondue pot and heat to a simmer over medium heat.

2. In a small cup, dissolve the cornstarch in 2 tablespoons of the Madeira and set aside.

3. Add the remaining Madeira, the butter, thyme, rosemary, and bay leaf to the fondue pot and simmer for 5 minutes.

4. Stir in the cornstarch mixture and whisk to thicken slightly. Taste and season with salt and pepper. Spear cubes of ham and dip into the bubbling broth to heat as desired.

Fall Cider Fondue

WHEN APPLES AND FRESH CIDER are at their peak in the fall, try this simple fondue. You'll have plenty of time to fuss with the condiments if you want to. Serve a homemade fresh apple chutney (recipe follows), sauerkraut, or coleslaw to accompany the pork.

● *Serves 6 (Makes about 4 cups)*

FONDUE POT: Large
DIPPERS: Pork cubes (see below)

2½ cups apple cider
2 cups Riesling
1 large shallot, minced
1 tablespoon minced fresh ginger
3 garlic cloves, minced
1½ pounds pork tenderloin, cut into ¾-inch cubes

1. Heat the cider, wine, shallot, ginger, and garlic in a large fondue pot over medium heat to a simmer. Simmer for 5 minutes. Maintain at a simmer for serving.

2. Spear and cook the pork cubes in the simmering broth for 3 to 4 minutes, or until white, firm, and cooked through.

Apple Chutney

This keeps well in the refrigerator for up to 2 weeks.

● *Makes 2 cups*

2 medium-size Rome Beauty or other red cooking apples
½ cup dried cranberries
¼ cup golden raisins
2 tablespoons light brown sugar
Zest of 1 orange
2 tablespoons apple cider vinegar
½ teaspoon ground cinnamon
¼ teaspoon ground cloves
¼ teaspoon ground nutmeg

1. Combine all of the ingredients in a medium-size saucepan. Bring to a simmer over medium-low heat. Cover and cook for 15 minutes or until the apples are soft.

2. Remove from the heat and let cool slightly. Transfer to a food processor and pulse into a very chunky puree.

Chocolate . . .
and Beyond

Chocolate . . . and Beyond

Chocolate Cappuccino Mint Fondue

BECOME AN EXPERT BARISTA in five minutes! Chocolate and coffee addicts alike will love any combination of fruit or crunchy cookies dipped in this rich and creamy chocolate pond. ● *Serves 6 (Makes 2¼ cups)*

FONDUE POT: Medium

DIPPERS: Soft dried apricots, sugar cookies, marshmallows, blackberries

1 pound bittersweet chocolate, chopped
½ cup heavy cream
3 tablespoons coffee liqueur
3 tablespoons peppermint schnapps or peppermint liqueur

1. Place the chocolate, cream, coffee liqueur, and peppermint schnapps in a medium-size fondue pot. Heat over medium-low heat until the mixture has melted together to form a very thick and smooth puree.

2. Serve over low heat.

Darkest Ever Chocolate Fondue

WIN OVER EVEN THE MOST JADED EATER by serving this fondue version of molten flourless chocolate cake. Use the darkest organic bittersweet eating chocolate you can find for the best flavor.

● *Serves 4 to 6 (Makes about 2 cups)*

FONDUE POT: Medium

DIPPERS: What can't you dip into this? Try fresh berries or other fruit, pretzels, pound cake cubes, baguette cubes, mini popcorn balls. . . .

11 ounces bittersweet chocolate, chopped
½ cup heavy cream
2 tablespoons orange liqueur, such as Grand Marnier
¼ teaspoon ground cinnamon, preferably Ceylon

1. Heat the chocolate, cream, orange liqueur, and cinnamon over medium heat in a medium-size fondue pot.

2. Serve warm using the lowest setting available on the fondue pot.

Natchez Chocolate Fondue

FIRST SAMPLED THIS FONDUE, one of the more indulgent recipes in this book, in Natchez, Mississippi. I suggest throwing calories and caution to the wind to enjoy this. Life is short. Do dessert. ● *Serves 4 (Makes 2¼ cups)*

FONDUE POT: Medium

DIPPERS: Plain cake doughnut pieces or holes, mini corn muffins, bread pudding squares

12 ounces semisweet baking chocolate

½ cup firmly packed light brown sugar

⅔ cup heavy cream

¼ cup (½ stick) cold unsalted butter, cut into cubes

¼ cup Jack Daniel's whiskey or bourbon

1. Heat the chocolate, brown sugar, cream, butter, and whiskey in a large fondue pot over the lowest possible heat setting, stirring frequently, until the mixture has melted and emulsified.

2. Serve the fondue over low heat.

S'mores Fondue

ANYONE WHO REMEMBERS a campfire and ghost stories in the woods remembers gooey, sweet, sticky, and luscious s'mores. Relive those times by melting all the ingredients in your fondue pot. Try to save some of the fondue, because as it cools and hardens it becomes a delectable, spoonable candy.

● Serves 6 (Makes 4 cups)

FONDUE POT: Large

DIPPERS: Plain, cinnamon, and chocolate graham crackers; marshmallows

One 14-ounce can sweetened condensed milk
12 ounces marshmallows, regular size or miniature
12 ounces semisweet chocolate chips
Pinch of sea salt
¾ cup graham cracker crumbs

1. Place the condensed milk, marshmallows, chocolate chips, and salt in a large fondue pot and heat over a very low setting until the marshmallows and chocolate melt, stirring frequently to form a creamy fondue. It is fine to have a few chunks of marshmallow remaining in the fondue as you serve it.

2. Stir in the graham cracker crumbs and serve the fondue on the lowest heat setting.

Chocolate Hazelnut Cheesecake Fondue

T HE FLAVOR OF THIS FONDUE reminds me of licking the bowl after putting a cheesecake into the oven. However, this treat is more forgiving than traditional cheesecake. Throw away worries of cracks, soggy crusts, and an iffy oven. Instead, just heat and serve this rich treat with a variety of dippers reminiscent of cheesecake crust. ● *Serves 6 (Makes 2¾ cups)*

FONDUE POT: Medium
DIPPERS: Graham crackers, sugar cookies, shortbread, biscuits

8½ ounces bittersweet chocolate, chopped
One 8-ounce package cream cheese, cubed
1 cup heavy cream
⅓ cup sugar
⅓ cup hazelnut liqueur
1 tablespoon pure vanilla extract

1. Place the chocolate, cream cheese, cream, sugar, liqueur, and vanilla in a medium-size fondue pot. Heat over a very low setting, stirring frequently, until the chocolate has melted.

2. Serve the fondue over low heat.

Guadalajara's Secret:
Mexican Abuelita Chocolate
Ganache Fondue

ONE, TWO, THREE, FONDUE! The secret here is in the type of chocolate used, which is fortified with cacao nibs, sugar, and cinnamon. All you do is melt it with a little help from the Mexican crema and the liqueur. If you have time to make homemade fried churros, they are excellent with the rich chocolate. ● *Serves 6 (Makes 2¼ cups)*

FONDUE POT: Medium
DIPPERS: Strawberries; tangerine, tangelo, and orange wedges;
    fresh pineapple cubes; Mexican wedding cookies; churros

**One 15-ounce container Cacique crema (Mexican table cream)
    or 2 cups heavy cream**
**One 12.6-ounce package sweet Mexican chocolate, such as
    Abuelita or Ibarra**
¼ cup hazelnut liqueur

1. Place the crema, chocolate, and liqueur in a medium-size fondue pot and heat on very low heat, stirring frequently, for 10 to 15 minutes, or until the chocolate is completely melted and the mixture is smooth and creamy.

2. Serve the fondue over low heat.

White Chocolate Marzipan Fondue

SWEET AND VOLUPTUOUS BEST describes this fetching fondue. You can serve it just barely warm with the macaroons, panettone, and strawberries, or serve it hot with the sponge cake and soft unglazed cookies.

● *Serves 8 (Makes 4 cups)*

FONDUE POT: Large
DIPPERS: Coconut macaroons, panettone, strawberries,
sponge cake cubes, soft sugar or chocolate chip cookies

1 pound white chocolate, chopped
2 ounces almond paste, chopped
½ cup half-and-half
¼ cup almond-flavored liqueur
1 teaspoon almond extract

1. Place the chocolate, almond paste, half-and-half, liqueur, and almond extract in a large fondue pot.

2. Cook for about 15 minutes over low heat to melt the chocolate and bring the mixture to a simmer. When the mixture is smooth and simmering, turn off the heat. The fondue will be thin. If desired, cool to room temperature. The fondue will thicken as it stands and cools. Serve either warm as a thin fondue glaze or cooled as a thicker dip.

Malted Peppermint Patty Fondue

FOR A SPECIAL EFFECT, float additional mini marshmallows on top of the fondue when serving it. This is great to make for a Halloween party when brisk evening temperatures bring silky hot chocolate to mind.

● Serves 4 (Makes 2 cups)

FONDUE POT: Medium
DIPPERS: Girl Scout Thin Mints, sweet biscuits, wafer cookies

1¼ cups mint chocolate chips
3 ounces miniature marshmallows
½ cup evaporated milk
2 tablespoons unsalted butter
1 tablespoon malted milk powder
Pinch of sea salt
½ cup half-and-half
½ cup finely chopped toasted almonds
3 tablespoons peppermint schnapps
1 tablespoon cornstarch
2 tablespoons water

1. Place the chocolate chips, marshmallows, evaporated milk, butter, malted milk powder, and salt in a medium-size fondue pot and heat over low heat until both the marshmallows and chocolate have melted and the mixture is smooth.

2. Stir in the half-and-half, almonds, and schnapps, and heat to a simmer.

3. Dissolve the cornstarch in the water and stir the mixture into the fondue.

4. Serve the fondue over low heat.

Creamy Zabaglione Fondue

THANKS GO TO JAY LONDON, my dear dessert-guru friend. His heavenly take on the classic zabaglione may seem like a bit of a stretch, as it is served just as the dessert is made, over a pot of simmering water! The taste is so remarkable, though, that you'll think it's just fine to serve this fondue in its double-boiler setup. ● *Serves 6 (Makes about 1½ cups)*

FONDUE POT: Medium

DIPPERS: Chunks of peach, nectarine, or plum; biscotti; ladyfingers; angel food cake or pound cake cubes

8 egg yolks
½ cup sugar
½ cup dry Marsala or sherry
½ cup heavy cream

1. Heat 2 inches of water in a 4-quart saucepan. Place all of the ingredients in a medium-size heatproof bowl that will fit over the saucepan without touching the water. Place the bowl over the saucepan and heat the contents of the bowl, beating with an electric hand mixer for 5 to 8 minutes or until the mixture thickens. The mixture will first foam and then thicken a few minutes later. The fondue will resemble a thick sauce. Cook until it reaches 120° to 130°F on an instant-read thermometer.

2. Fill a medium-size fondue pot with 2 inches of water and heat to a simmer. Place the bowl of warm zabaglione over the fondue pot and serve, keeping the water in the pot at the barest simmer to avoid cooking the egg yolks.

Tiramisu Fondue

TAKE YOUR FONDEST TIRAMISU MEMORIES and heat them in a fondue pot, for the best tiramisu you've yet to taste. This is unique. Serve rich espresso alongside. ● *Serves 6 (Makes about 3 cups)*

FONDUE POT: Medium
DIPPERS: Homemade or store-bought Italian ladyfingers

One 8-ounce container mascarpone cheese
One 8-ounce container ricotta cheese
1 cup heavy cream
¾ cup sugar
3 tablespoons amaretto or gold rum
1 tablespoon instant espresso granules
1 tablespoon cornstarch
2 tablespoons water

1. Heat the cheeses, cream, sugar, amaretto, and espresso granules in a medium size fondue pot over the lowest heat setting, stirring frequently.

2. Dissolve the cornstarch in the water. When the mixture in the fondue pot has melted and the texture is smooth and creamy, stir in the cornstarch mixture and whisk until the fondue is slightly thick.

3. Serve the fondue over low heat.

Caramel Rum Fondue

CARAMEL APPLES are dipped to order here! Revisit those memories of caramel apples at Halloween, but this time as an adult treat with rum and cream. Feel free to use flavored rum if you like.

● *Serves 4 to 6 (Makes 2½ cups)*

FONDUE POT: Medium

DIPPERS: Any tart apple wedges, such as Granny Smith or Macoun

2½ cups sugar
1 cup water
1¾ cups heavy cream
3 tablespoons dark rum
Pinch of sea salt

1. Place the sugar and water in a heavy saucepan and heat over medium-high heat to a boil. Cook until the syrup caramelizes, 10 to 15 minutes. During this time, the syrup will thicken and eventually turn a dark amber color. Remove from the heat.

2. Carefully stir in the cream, rum, and salt. The mixture will instantly form large clumps of sugar. Reheat the mixture over low heat until the caramel is thick and the sugar clumps have dissolved.

3. Transfer to a medium-size fondue pot and serve over the lowest heat setting.

Tres Leches Fondue

CAJETA, A TYPE OF CONDENSED GOAT'S MILK, is traditionally used as an ingredient in the icing on a *tres leches* cake. It's easy to make; however, if schedules are tight, then just substitute plain goat's milk, heavy cream, or a combination of the two. Vanilla sugar is readily available in many supermarkets and specialty stores, but you can easily make your own by splitting a large vanilla bean and burying it in a jar filled with 2 to 3 cups of sugar. Leave the jar in a cool spot and within a few weeks the sugar will be extremely aromatic and infused with vanilla flavor. ● *Serves 6 (Makes 2½ cups)*

FONDUE POT: Medium
DIPPERS: Cubes of banana bread, lemon cake, or pound cake;
  sugar cookies; shortbread

One 14-ounce can coconut milk
One 14-ounce can sweetened condensed milk
½ cup *cajeta* (recipe follows), goat's milk, or heavy cream
½ cup vanilla sugar
¼ cup coconut rum
1 tablespoon cornstarch
2 tablespoons water
1 cup flaked sweetened coconut, lightly toasted

1. Place a medium-size fondue pot over very low heat and heat the coconut milk, condensed milk, *cajeta,* vanilla sugar, and rum to a simmer.

2. Dissolve the cornstarch in the water and add the mixture to the fondue pot, add the coconut, and stir constantly until the fondue thickens slightly.

3. Serve the fondue over low heat.

Cajeta

This can be made several days in advance if desired.

● *Makes ¾ cup*

1½ cups goat's milk
½ cup firmly packed light brown sugar
1 tablespoon water
1½ teaspoons honey
½ teaspoon baking soda

Place the milk, brown sugar, water, honey, and baking soda in a medium-size sauce-pan and heat to a simmer. Cook for about 25 minutes over low heat until the mixture has thickened and reduced by half. Use immediately, or cool and refrigerate.

Cuban Mojito Fondue

THIS FONDUE proves to be the cooling formula for a hot and humid evening by the sea. If you can find peppermint oil, use a few drops of it rather than fresh mint, which, although tasty, may darken as the fondue continues to heat. If you can't find Key limes, regular (Persian) limes are fine, too.

● *Serves 4 (Makes 2 cups)*

FONDUE POT: Medium
DIPPERS: Coconut cookies, dried coconut chips, fresh coconut chunks, fresh pineapple cubes, sweet biscuits

1¼ cups heavy cream, plus more if needed
½ cup sugar, plus more if desired
¼ cup freshly squeezed Key lime juice
¼ cup Cuban dark rum, plus more if needed
2 tablespoons chopped fresh mint
1 tablespoon cornstarch
2 tablespoons water or heavy cream

1. Place the cream, sugar, lime juice, rum, and mint in a medium-size fondue pot and heat over low heat, stirring frequently.

2. Dissolve the cornstarch in the water or cream. Whisk the mixture into the fondue. Taste and add additional sugar if desired.

3. Serve the fondue over low heat, thinning as needed with additional cream or rum.

Peanut Butter Delightful Fondue

ERE'S A HOT, CREAMY peanut butter shake disguised as fondue. Feel free to substitute any nut butter, such as almond, cashew, or macadamia nut. And here's a bonus: Leftovers are scrumptious for several days afterward. Use them to cheer up a basic PB&J sandwich or on pancakes or waffles.

● *Serves 8 (Makes about 4½ cups)*

FONDUE POT: Large
DIPPERS: Unfrosted mini cupcakes, madeleines, coconut cookies, thick banana slices

One 16-ounce jar creamy peanut butter (do not use natural peanut butter)
1⅔ cups half-and-half or milk, plus more if needed
One 8-ounce package cream cheese, cubed
2 tablespoons amaretto or coconut rum

1. Place the peanut butter, half-and-half, cream cheese, and amaretto in a large fondue pot and melt over very low heat for 15 minutes, stirring frequently, until the mixture is smooth and thick.

2. Serve the fondue on the lowest heat setting, thinning as needed with additional half-and-half.

Thanksgiving Pumpkin Pie Fondue

PROLONG THE PLEASURE OF THANKSGIVING, or any winter holiday party for that matter, with this divine fantasy. If you serve this on Thanksgiving, make sure to include piecrust sticks for those diehard pie fans. This is a sure a way to extend your time at the holiday table and catch up on the year's events. ● *Serves 6 to 8 (Makes about 5½ cups)*

FONDUE POT: Large
DIPPERS: Sugar cookies, graham crackers, shortbread, gingersnaps, baked piecrust sticks

2 cups heavy cream
One 15-ounce can pumpkin puree
One 8-ounce package cream cheese, cubed
8 ounces mascarpone cheese
¾ cup firmly packed light or dark brown sugar
¼ cup amaretto
1 tablespoon pure vanilla extract
1 teaspoon ground cinnamon
½ teaspoon ground nutmeg
½ teaspoon ground mace
1 tablespoon cornstarch
2 tablespoons water

1. Place the cream, pumpkin, cheeses, brown sugar, amaretto, vanilla, cinnamon, nutmeg, and mace in a large fondue pot. Heat over medium-low heat, stirring frequently as the cheeses melt.

2. When the fondue is smooth and warm, dissolve the cornstarch in the water and whisk the mixture into the fondue.

3. Serve the fondue over medium-low heat.

Kir Royale Fondue

SERVED WARM OR COLD, this is a class act fit for a grand finale to any special occasion. For a refined version, strain out the seeds after pureeing the raspberry mixture and serve the fondue with classic French madeleines and fresh raspberries. ● *Serves 6 (Makes about 4 cups)*

FONDUE POT: Large

DIPPERS: Ripe melon cubes, peaches, nectarines,
soft dried sweetened cranberries, chocolate cookies,
madeleines, fresh raspberries

Two 12-ounce packages unsweetened frozen raspberries, thawed
½ cup firmly packed light brown sugar
½ cup sparkling rosé wine
3 tablespoons crème de cassis
1 tablespoon freshly squeezed lemon juice
1½ teaspoons lemon zest

1. Place the berries in a blender. Add the sugar, wine, crème de cassis, lemon juice, and lemon zest and blend into a puree.

2. Pour the mixture into a large fondue pot and heat over very low heat. Serve slightly warm.

Cinq Amandes Fondue

WHERE'S THE CREAM? When taste-testing this quintuple-whammy almond fondue, it was impossible to believe that it was completely nondairy. Almond lovers will swoon over the light but intense almond scent and flavor. ● *Serves 6 (Makes 4 cups)*

FONDUE POT: Large
DIPPERS: Sweet biscuits, wafer cookies, pound cake or brownie cubes

1¼ cups raw almonds
2 cups chocolate-flavored almond milk, plus more if needed
4½ ounces soft almond paste, cut into small pieces
¼ cup sugar
¼ cup amaretto
2 ounces unsweetened chocolate
½ teaspoon almond extract

1. Preheat the oven to 350°F. Place the almonds on a baking sheet and toast for 10 to 12 minutes. Let cool slightly, then grind to a fine paste in a spice grinder or food processor.

2. Place the ground almonds, almond milk, almond paste, sugar, amaretto, chocolate, and almond extract in a large fondue pot and heat over low heat. Stir the mixture frequently as the chocolate melts and the fondue becomes smooth.

3. Serve over low heat, thinning the mixture as necessary with almond milk.

Fall Applesauce Fondue

IF YOU CAN FIND THEM, use firm and juicy Golden Delicious apples for this dessert fondue. Of course, any combination of apples will work, especially during the fall apple season when lots of varieties can be readily found.

● *Serves 4 to 6 (Makes 2 ½ cups)*

FONDUE POT: Medium

DIPPERS: Firm Brie cheese cubes, shortbread, sugar cookies

3 medium-size firm apples, cored and chopped
1 cup apple juice or cider
2 tablespoons brandy or orange liqueur
1 tablespoon vanilla sugar (page 158)
1 tablespoon finely minced fresh ginger
Zest of 1 small lemon
1½ teaspoons ground cinnamon
Pinch of sea salt
½ cup heavy cream
3 tablespoons unsalted butter

1. Place the apples, apple juice, brandy, vanilla sugar, ginger, lemon zest, cinnamon, and salt in a medium-size saucepan and heat over medium heat until the mixture boils. Reduce the heat to a simmer, cover, and cook for 25 minutes.

2. When the apples are very soft, remove from the heat and cool the mixture for 5 minutes. Transfer the mixture to a blender or food processor and puree until smooth.

3. Place the pureed mixture in a large fondue pot and stir in the cream and butter.

4. Serve the fondue on the lowest heat setting.

Bananas Foster Fondue

NAMED FOR RICHARD FOSTER, who was chief officer of the local crime commission in New Orleans and a frequent customer of Brennan's Restaurant, Bananas Foster was designed for and dedicated to him by Brennan's chef in the 1950s. For the best effect, make the whole fondue tableside. Be sure to let guests dip a few bananas into the classic sauce before adding the ice cream. ● *Serves 6 (Makes 4 cups)*

FONDUE POT: Large
DIPPERS: Banana chunks, wafer cookies, sugar cookies

¾ **cup firmly packed light brown sugar**
3 **tablespoons unsalted butter**
1½ **teaspoons ground cinnamon**
¼ **cup banana liqueur**
2 **medium-size bananas, peeled and minced**
¼ **cup dark or gold rum**
2 **cups vanilla ice cream, softened**

1. Heat the brown sugar, butter, and cinnamon in a large fondue pot over medium-low heat. Cook for 1 minute.

2. Add the banana liqueur and heat to a simmer. Stir in the minced bananas and cook for 5 minutes, stirring frequently. Stir in the rum and heat until the mixture becomes a thickened sauce.

3. Stir in the ice cream until thoroughly blended. Serve the fondue over low heat.

State Fair Fondue

BANANAS ON A STICK are a state fair mainstay in many areas of the country. For the fondue version, choose firm bananas for dipping, as they will be easier to spear and dip into the chocolate and granola crumbs. Designer granola and artisan chocolate will elevate this humble old-time dip into a treat worthy of any gourmet. ● *Serves 6 (Makes about 1½ cups)*

FONDUE POT: Medium
DIPPERS: Banana chunks

2 cups crushed granola
¼ cup plus 2 tablespoons unsalted butter, melted
12 ounces bittersweet chocolate, chopped
½ cup heavy cream

1. Preheat the oven to 350°F. Place the granola crumbs in a small baking pan and pour the ¼ cup melted butter over them. Stir until the crumbs are coated. Bake for 10 minutes, or until they are slightly golden. Remove to a serving bowl and let cool.

2. Heat the remaining 2 tablespoons melted butter, the chocolate, and cream in a medium-size fondue pot, stirring to thoroughly mix in the butter.

3. Serve the fondue with a platter of banana chunks for dipping and one large or several small bowls of granola crumbs to roll the dipped bananas in.

Liquid Lemon Curd Fondue

THIS IS ONE FONDUE that is as good cold as it is warm, so if you should be fortunate enough have some left over, try it on morning toast or as an addition to a tart or pie filling. ● *Serves 6 (Makes about 1¼ cups)*

FONDUE POT: Large
DIPPERS: Cubes of citrus-flavored or vanilla pound cake or
    angel food cake; fresh berries; ladyfingers; orange, tangerine,
    or clementine wedges

2 large eggs plus 1 large egg yolk
½ cup heavy cream
½ cup sugar
¼ cup freshly squeezed lemon juice
¼ cup freshly squeezed orange juice
2 tablespoons limoncello
2 teaspoons finely grated lemon zest
2 teaspoons finely grated orange zest

1. Bring 3 inches of water in a 3- or 4-quart saucepan to a simmer. Place all of the ingredients in a medium-size heatproof bowl that will fit over the saucepan without touching the water. Gently whisk the ingredients for 5 to 8 minutes. The fondue mixture will begin to thicken when the temperature is at 130°F (check using an instant-read thermometer). Continue to whisk as the mixture continues to thicken, another 10 minutes or so. The temperature will reach 150°F and the fondue will resemble a thick sauce. Remove the fondue from the heat.

2. Set up a large fondue pot with just a few inches of water in the pot and bring to a simmer. With the heat on the lowest possible setting, place the bowl of fondue over the fondue pot to serve. If the heat is kept at a very low setting, the fondue will remain at a perfect dipping consistency for at least 30 minutes. The mixture will continue to thicken as it cooks.

Melon Medley with Blackberry Cassis Fondue

U SE THE JUICE of any dark fresh berry for this treat, and serve a glass of bubbly to accompany it. Keep the bottle close by the pot and use the bubbly both to thin the fondue as needed and to refresh the flutes!

● *Serves 4 (Makes 2 cups)*

FONDUE POT: Medium

DIPPERS: Chunks of ripe summer melon, such as cantaloupe, muskmelon, honeydew, or Crenshaw

1 pint fresh blackberries
2 tablespoons crème de cassis
¾ cup unsweetened blackberry juice
⅓ cup confectioners' sugar
Pinch of sea salt
1 tablespoon cornstarch
2 tablespoons water

1. Place the blackberries and crème de cassis in a blender and puree until smooth.

2. Place the puree in a medium-size fondue pot. Stir in the juice, confectioners' sugar, and salt and heat the mixture over medium-low heat.

3. Dissolve the cornstarch in the water. When the fondue has reached a simmer, stir in the cornstarch mixture until the fondue has thickened slightly.

4. Serve the fondue over medium-low heat.

Caramel Mocha Fondue

M ADE WITH JUST A FEW INGREDIENTS, this caramelized coffee treat in a fondue pot has a taste that is remarkable. Serve small cups of espresso along with the suggested dippers.

● *Serves 8 (Makes about 6 cups)*

FONDUE POT: Large
DIPPERS: Chocolate and vanilla wafer cookies, other
   vanilla-flavored cookies, sponge cake cubes

½ cup sugar
2 teaspoons water
1½ quarts coffee ice cream, softened
¼ cup coffee liqueur
2 ounces unsweetened chocolate

1. Place the sugar and water in a large fondue pot and heat over medium heat until the mixture is a deep amber color, taking care to avoid stirring as it cooks. Let cool only slightly before adding the ice cream. The mixture will bubble up and the caramel will harden.

2. Stir in the liqueur and chocolate and heat over low heat to melt the chocolate and re-melt the caramel.

3. Serve the fondue over low heat.

Chai Latte Fondue

THIS FONDUE WILL PLEASE the tea lovers in your crowd. Feel free to use any type of spiced chai tea in the fondue, and be sure to include either crumpet or scone cubes as well as mini ginger muffins for dippers. A hot pot of mulled wine goes well with this fondue at holiday time.

● *Serves 6 (Makes 4½ cups)*

FONDUE POT: Large
DIPPERS: Scone chunks, mini ginger muffins, tea biscuits,
    cubes of nut cake and fruitcake

4 spiced chai tea bags
3⅓ cups water
¼ cup firmly packed light brown sugar
1 cup heavy cream
2 teaspoons pure vanilla extract
One 8-ounce package cream cheese, cubed
3 tablespoons cornstarch

1. Place the tea bags, 3 cups of the water, and the brown sugar in a saucepan over medium heat. When the mixture begins to simmer, remove from the heat, cover the pot, and let the tea steep for 5 minutes. Remove and discard the tea bags. Stir in the cream and vanilla.

2. Place the chai in a large fondue pot. Add the cream cheese and heat over medium-low heat. When the mixture begins to simmer, dissolve the cornstarch in the remaining ⅓ cup water and stir the mixture into the fondue. Whisk the mixture until it begins to thicken.

3. Serve on the lowest heat setting.

Pride of the Port Fondue

ALITTLE GOES A LONG WAY with this very rich fondue heavily laced with good port wine. Serve small glasses of your favorite vintage port to accompany this, and add the same elixir to the pot. Serve simple, plain dippers to showcase this extravagant treat. ● *Serves 6 (Makes 2 cups)*

FONDUE POT: Medium
DIPPERS: Cream biscuits, not-too-sweet cookies, plain madeleines

10 ounces extra-dark bittersweet chocolate
¾ cup port
⅓ cup heavy cream
2 tablespoons unsalted butter
Pinch of sea salt

1. Place the chocolate, port, cream, butter, and salt in a medium-size fondue pot and heat over medium-low heat, stirring frequently until the chocolate has melted and the fonduc is smooth and creamy.

2. Serve the fondue over low heat.

Silky Cranberry Fondue with Calvados

THIS BEAUTIFUL scarlet-colored liquid jam is heady with apple liquor. What a lovely alternative to traditional holiday desserts. Should you be blessed with leftover fondue, try spooning it over eggnog ice cream.

● *Serves 6 (Makes 3 cups)*

FONDUE POT: Medium

DIPPERS: A variety of apple slices, pound cake cubes, pumpkin bread cubes

2¼ cups sweetened cranberry juice
1 cup dried cranberries
Zest of 1 orange
¼ cup Calvados
2 tablespoons cornstarch

1. Place the juice and dried cranberries in a medium-size fondue pot and let steep for at least 4 hours or overnight.

2. Remove and reserve ¼ cup of the juice. Add the orange zest and Calvados to the fondue pot and heat until the mixture begins to simmer. Cook on the lowest heat setting for 5 minutes.

3. Dissolve the cornstarch in the reserved juice and stir the mixture into the bubbling fondue. Whisk to thoroughly blend, and continue stirring until the fondue thickens.

4. Serve the fondue on the lowest heat setting.

Holiday Eggnog Fondue

TAKE CARE TO PREPARE THIS on the lowest possible heat setting to avoid ending up with scrambled eggs. For a classic presentation, whip the 3 unused egg whites and gently place them on top of the fondue as it simmers so that they poach. ● *Serves 6 (Makes 3½ cups)*

FONDUE POT: Medium
DIPPERS: Unfilled mini cream puffs, holiday sugar cookies,
     cubes of lemon cake or poppyseed cake

3 large egg yolks
⅓ cup granulated sugar
1 tablespoon vanilla sugar (page 158)
2 cups half-and-half
1 cup heavy cream
¼ teaspoon ground nutmeg
3 tablespoons cornstarch
¼ cup bourbon or brandy

1. Place the egg yolks and the sugars in a medium-size fondue pot and whisk together until the mixture is light, about 3 minutes. Add the half-and-half, cream, and nutmeg and heat over the lowest possible heat setting until the eggnog begins to simmer.

2. Dissolve the cornstarch in the bourbon and whisk the mixture into the fondue. Continue whisking until the eggnog thickens, 2 to 4 minutes.

3. Serve the fondue on the lowest possible heat setting.

Hot Buttered Rum Fondue

EXPECTING A CROWD after being on the ski slopes all day? Serve this fondue and sweet dippers for a wonderful alternative to the standard après-ski fare. Of course, the fondue is also an exquisite winter dessert that will warm up the coldest of evenings at home. ● *Serves 6 (Makes 4½ cups)*

FONDUE POT: Large
DIPPERS: Cinnamon graham crackers, wafer cookies,
almond cookies, French-style macarons

⅓ cup cornstarch
1 pint vanilla ice cream, softened
1 cup firmly packed light brown sugar
¼ cup (½ stick) unsalted butter
2 teaspoons ground cinnamon
¼ teaspoon ground nutmeg
Pinch of sea salt
Pinch of ground cloves
1½ cups dark rum

1. Place the cornstarch in a small bowl and stir in ½ cup of the softened ice cream to dissolve the cornstarch.

2. Place the brown sugar and butter in a large fondue pot and heat over low heat. When the butter has melted and the sugar begins to dissolve, stir in the cinnamon, nutmeg, salt, and cloves. Cook over the lowest setting for 5 minutes.

3. Stir in the rum and the remaining 1½ cups ice cream. Heat to a simmer over low heat. Stir in the dissolved cornstarch and whisk until thickened.

4. Serve the fondue over low heat.

Roca Fondue

DURING THE HOLIDAYS, Almond Roca candy flies off the shelves in the supermarket. At other times of the year, Mocha Roca is easy to find. Either way, the candy provides a crunchiness in this fondue that is unexpected and lots of fun. It's a treat for children as well as grownups, so keep the dippers fun for all ages. ● *Serves 4 (Makes 3 cups)*

FONDUE POT: Medium
DIPPERS: Animal crackers, marshmallows, chocolate chip cookies

4 ounces Almond Roca, Mocha Roca, or Heath bar candy, chopped
1 cup heavy cream
1 cup sweetened condensed milk
⅓ cup sugar
2 teaspoons pure vanilla extract
½ teaspoon almond extract
2 large eggs

1. Place the candy, cream, condensed milk, sugar, and vanilla and almond extracts in a medium-size fondue pot over medium-low heat. Stir frequently until the candy has melted.

2. Place the eggs in a small bowl and beat them. Stir in ½ cup of the warm cream mixture. Blend well, then add the mixture to the fondue pot and stir to combine.

3. Serve on the lowest possible heat setting.

Nuttin' Honey Fondue

ANY TYPE OF NUTS, including almonds, pecans, or macadamias, can be used in this super-fast and light fondue. Just make sure to have a matching liqueur to keep the nut flavor pure and intense. It's also a good idea to serve dippers such as cookies and nut bread cubes with the same flavor as the nuts you use in the fondue. ● *Serves 4 (Makes 2½ cups)*

FONDUE POT: Medium
DIPPERS: Pear and banana slices, hazelnut pound cake cubes,
   hazelnut cookies

1 cup hazelnuts
12 ounces semisweet chocolate chips
¼ cup hazelnut liqueur
3 tablespoons honey
2 tablespoons unsalted butter
1 cup half-and-half

1. Heat the oven to 350°F. Place the hazelnuts on a baking sheet and bake for 10 to 12 minutes. Remove from the oven, cool the nuts slightly, place them in a spice grinder or food processor, and grind into a smooth paste.

2. Place the nut paste, chocolate chips, liqueur, honey, and butter in a medium-size fondue pot and heat over low heat until the chocolate melts.

3. Whisk in the half-and-half, stirring until the mixture is smooth and creamy.

4. Serve the fondue over low heat.

Rice Pudding Fondue

THIS THICK, HEARTY FONDUE is great for a casual crowd on a cozy winter evening. Feel free to substitute golden raisins or dried blueberries for the cranberries. As the pudding sits, it will thicken considerably, so keep a pitcher of warm cream or milk close by to thin the fondue as needed.

● *Serves 6 (Makes 3 cups)*

FONDUE POT: Large
DIPPERS: Wafer cookies, tea biscuits, gingersnaps,
   graham crackers, shortbread

½ cup dried cranberries
2 tablespoons gold rum
1½ cups cooked jasmine rice
1½ cups milk
⅓ cup firmly packed light brown sugar
2 tablespoons unsalted butter
2 teaspoons pure vanilla extract
1 teaspoon ground cinnamon
Pinch of sea salt
½ cup heavy cream
1 large egg, beaten

1. Place the cranberries in a small microwave-safe bowl and pour the rum over them. Cover the dish and microwave for 20 to 30 seconds or until steaming. Let cool before removing the cover. Alternatively, the cranberries can be soaked in the rum for a few hours until plumped.

2. Place the rice, milk, brown sugar, butter, vanilla, cinnamon, and salt in a large fondue pot and heat over medium-low heat. Simmer the mixture for 5 minutes.

3. Stir in the cream, egg, and cranberry-rum mixture, whisking until the fondue thickens slightly.

4. Serve the fondue over low heat.

Rice Rêve Fondue

A DREAMY DESSERT CUSTOM-MADE FOR the nondairy crowd, this rice milk–based fondue is beautifully creamy and smooth. Aseptic containers of rice milk, which can be stored in the pantry, are a marvelous ingredient to keep on hand for this treat, as well as for most other times when a substitute for milk is required. ● *Serves 6 (Makes 2½ cups)*

FONDUE POT: Medium
DIPPERS: Hazelnut rusks, fresh berries, thick banana slices

2 cups vanilla or hazelnut rice milk
¾ cup coconut milk
¾ cup hazelnut liqueur
¼ cup firmly packed dark brown sugar
1 tablespoon vanilla sugar (page 158)
¼ teaspoon sea salt
3 ounces unsweetened chocolate, chopped
3 tablespoons cornstarch
⅓ cup water

1. Place the rice milk, coconut milk, liqueur, sugars, and salt in a medium-size fondue pot and heat over medium heat. Reduce the heat to low and stir in the chocolate.

2. Dissolve the cornstarch in the water. When the chocolate has melted and the fondue is smooth, stir in the cornstarch mixture and simmer over low heat until thickened.

3. Serve the fondue over low heat.

Butterscotch-Almond Fondue

F YOU'RE LOOKING FOR a decadent nondairy dessert fondue, give this light and lovely meltdown using soy milk a try. The caramel adds a three-star dimension that will thrill any guest. ● *Serves 6 (Makes 2½ cups)*

FONDUE POT: Medium
DIPPERS: Strawberries, melon cubes, chocolate or
   vanilla cookies, sponge cake cubes, granola bar pieces

½ **cup raw almonds**
1 **cup sugar**
2 **tablespoons water**
1½ **cups soy milk**
3 **tablespoons amaretto**
1 **tablespoon pure vanilla extract**
1 **tablespoon unsweetened cocoa powder**
½ **teaspoon almond extract**

1. Heat the oven to 350°F. Place the almonds on a baking sheet and bake for 10 to 12 minutes, or until the almonds are hot to the touch. Cool the nuts slightly, place them in a spice grinder or food processor, and grind into a fine paste.

2. Heat the sugar and water together over the highest heat setting in a medium-size fondue pot. Avoid stirring. When the mixture has melted and has turned a golden amber color, turn the heat off for 5 minutes.

3. Reheat over medium-low heat and add the soy milk, amaretto, vanilla, cocoa powder, ground almonds, and almond extract. Cook until the mixture is smooth. Note that the sugar may have hardened slightly; it will resoften as it heats.

4. Serve the fondue over low heat.

Just Peachy Sangria Fondue

WITH ITS PALE GOLDEN COLOR and silky thin consistency, this winey adult dessert, although warm, is extremely refreshing on a very hot summer night. Any leftovers are delicious when frozen and eaten "slushy" style. ● *Serves 6 (Makes 3 cups)*

FONDUE POT: Medium

DIPPERS: All types of stone fruits, such as white and yellow peaches, nectarines, and plums, cubed; biscuits; cream crackers

12 ounces white peaches (about 3 large peaches)
2 cups dry white wine
¼ cup freshly squeezed orange juice
Zest of 1 orange
4½ teaspoons freshly squeezed lime juice
2 tablespoons cornstarch
¼ cup peach schnapps or any color rum

1. Peel the peaches, cut them in half, remove the pits, and puree them in a food processor or blender.

2. Heat the peaches, wine, orange juice, orange zest, and lime juice in a medium-size fondue pot over medium-low heat until the mixture begins to boil. Reduce the heat to the lowest heat setting.

3. Dissolve the cornstarch in the schnapps and stir the mixture into the fondue. Continue to stir until the fondue thickens slightly.

4. Serve the fondue over medium-low heat.

Turkish Coffee Fondue

ROSE SYRUP, with its distinctive yet only slightly floral taste, can be found in Middle Eastern groceries as well as specialty stores. (This is a thick, sweetened syrup that is different from rose water.) Lovers of strong coffee will appreciate the rich and robust flavor of this thick sauce.

● *Serves 6 (Makes 3 cups)*

FONDUE POT: Medium
DIPPERS: Nut biscotti, sesame cookies, sweet biscuits, chocolate cookies

1½ cups milk
1 cup heavy cream
½ cup French-roast coffee beans
½ cup sugar
1 tablespoon rose syrup
Pinch of sea salt
2 tablespoons cornstarch
¼ cup cognac

1. Heat the milk, cream, coffee beans, sugar, rose syrup, and salt in a medium-size saucepan until the mixture just begins to simmer. Cool, cover, and let the beans steep in the liquid for 2 to 4 hours at room temperature or in the refrigerator for 1 day.

2. Strain the mixture into a medium-size fondue pot and heat over the lowest heat setting.

3. Dissolve the cornstarch in the cognac. When the fondue is simmering, whisk in the cornstarch mixture and continue to whisk until the fondue has thickened.

4. Serve on the lowest heat setting.

Measurement Equivalents

Please note that all conversions are approximate.

Liquid Conversions

U.S.	Metric
1 tsp	5 ml
1 tbs	15 ml
2 tbs	30 ml
3 tbs	45 ml
¼ cup	60 ml
⅓ cup	75 ml
⅓ cup + 1 tbs	90 ml
⅓ cup + 2 tbs	100 ml
½ cup	120 ml
⅔ cup	150 ml
¾ cup	180 ml
¾ cup + 2 tbs	200 ml

U.S.	Metric
1 cup	240 ml
1 cup + 2 tbs	275 ml
1¼ cups	300 ml
1⅓ cups	325 ml
1½ cups	350 ml
1⅔ cups	375 ml
1¾ cups	400 ml
1¾ cups + 2 tbs	450 ml
2 cups (1 pint)	475 ml
2½ cups	600 ml
3 cups	720 ml
4 cups (1 quart)	945 ml

(1,000 ml is 1 liter)

Weight Conversions

U.S. / U.K.	Metric	U.S. / U.K.	Metric
1/2 oz	14 g	7 oz	200 g
1 oz	28 g	8 oz	227 g
1 1/2 oz	43 g	9 oz	255 g
2 oz	57 g	10 oz	284 g
2 1/2 oz	71 g	11 oz	312 g
3 oz	85 g	12 oz	340 g
3 1/2 oz	100 g	13 oz	368 g
4 oz	113 g	14 oz	400 g
5 oz	142 g	15 oz	425 g
6 oz	170 g	1 lb	454 g

Oven Temperature Conversions

°F	Gas Mark	°C
250	1/2	120
275	1	140
300	2	150
325	3	165
350	4	180
375	5	190
400	6	200
425	7	220
450	8	230
475	9	240
500	10	260
550	Broil	290

Index of Dippers

General Index

Get the most out of your slow cooker

with these best-selling Not Your Mother's® cookbooks!

Not Your Mother's Slow Cooker Cookbook

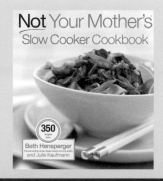

Chili, Olive, and Cheese Casserole • Slow-Steamed Artichokes • Provençal Garlic Soup • Ratatouille • Chicken Cacciatore • Pork Ribs with Molasses Glaze • Duck Breasts with Port Wine Sauce • Crock-Baked Apples • Hot Fudge Spoon Cake

Not Your Mother's Slow Cooker Recipes for Two

Red Wine Risotto with Mushrooms • Chipotle Black Bean Vegetable Soup • Marinara and Mozzarella Lasagna • Pork Tenderloin with Ginger-Plum Glaze • Glazed Whole Baby Ham with Pineapple • Cabernet Short Ribs of Beef with Apricots • Slow Cooker Buttermilk Biscuit Dumplings

Not Your Mother's Slow Cooker Recipes for Entertaining

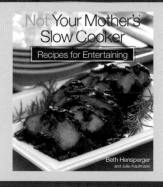

Champagne Fondue • Welsh Rabbit • Plum Sauce Chicken Wings • Beef Stroganoff with Porcini Mushrooms • Cherry-Glazed Pork Pot Roast with Herbs • Chili Colorado • Slow-Poached Pears with Warm Chocolate Sauce • Raspberry Truffles • Mulled Wine

Not Your Mother's Slow Cooker Family Favorites

Irish Oatmeal with Vanilla and Maple • Crustless Bacon and Broccoli Quiche • Not Your Mother's Chicken Noodle Soup • Tarragon Chicken in Mushroom Sauce with Simply Delicious Oven-Baked Rice • Twice-Crocked Stuffed Potatoes with Artichokes and Parmesan • Sweet and Sour Country Ribs

www.notyourmotherscookbooks.com

Short on time?
Fix dinner in a flash
with these exciting additions to the Not Your Mother's® series!

Not Your Mother's Weeknight Cooking

Turkey or Chicken Marsala with Olive Couscous • Sake Swordfish with Asian Greens • Chinese Dumpling Soup with Shiitake Mushrooms, Greens, and Tofu • Lemon Chicken with Mint • Duck Breast Salad with Blueberries, Walnuts, and Currant Vinaigrette • Horseradish Meatloaf • The Great White Vegetable and Garlic Pizza

Not Your Mother's Microwave Cookbook

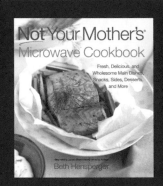

Masala Chai • Pesto Shrimp Pasta • Broccoli and Cheese–Stuffed Potatoes • Spinach-Artichoke Dip • Cup of Miso • Not Your Mother's Risotto with Asparagus and Mushrooms • Steamed Catfish with Ginger • Chicken Curry for One • Mini Meatloaves • Dark Chocolate Peppermint Bark

Coming in January 2011

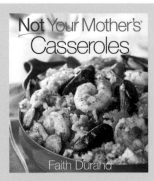

Not Your Mother's Casseroles

Lemon Brioche French Toast • Roasted Shrimp and Tomatoes with Basil • Pesto and Goat Cheese Baked Rounds • Roasted Carrots with Lemon, Feta, and Mint • Spanish Saffron Pilaf • Spicy Mexican Bean and Rice Bake • Oven Paella with Chicken, Shrimp, and Chorizo • Easy Payoff Oven Short Ribs • No-Bake Boston Cream Pie Strata

www.notyourmotherscookbooks.com